The Mindfulness & Acceptance Workbook for Bulimia

A Guide to Breaking Free from Bulimia
Using Acceptance & Commitment Therapy

EMILY K. SANDOZ, PhD
KELLY G. WILSON, PhD • TROY DUFRENE

New Harbinger Publications, Inc.

Distributed in Canada by Raincoast Books

Copyright © 2011 by Emily K. Sandoz, Kelly G. Wilson, and Troy DuFrene
New Harbinger Publications, Inc.
5674 Shattuck Avenue
Oakland, CA 94609
www.newharbinger.com

Cover design by Amy Shoup
Acquired by Catharine Meyers
Edited by Heather Garnos

Library of Congress Cataloging-in-Publication Data

Sandoz, Emily K.
   The mindfulness and acceptance workbook for bulimia : a guide to breaking free from bulimia using acceptance and commitment therapy / Emily K. Sandoz, Kelly G. Wilson, and Troy DuFrene.
       p. cm.
   Includes bibliographical references.
   ISBN 978-1-57224-735-2 (pbk.) -- ISBN 978-1-57224-739-0 (pdf ebook)
   1. Bulimia--Treatment--Problems, exercises, etc. 2. Bulimia--Psychological aspects--Problems, exercises, etc. 3. Acceptance and commitment therapy--Problems, exercises, etc. I. Wilson, Kelly G. II. DuFrene, Troy, 1972- III. Title.
   RC552.B84S26 2011
   616.85'263--dc22
                           2011007126

18   17   16

10   9   8   7   6   5   4   3   2

Contents

Dear reader,

Welcome to New Harbinger Publications. New Harbinger is dedicated to publishing books based on acceptance and commitment therapy (ACT) and its application to specific areas. New Harbinger has a long-standing reputation as a publisher of quality, well-researched books for general and professional audiences.

As part of New Harbinger's commitment to publishing books based on sound, scientific, clinical research, we oversee all prospective books for the Acceptance and Commitment Therapy Series. Serving as series editors, we comment on proposals and offer guidance as needed, and use a gentle hand in making suggestions regarding the content, depth, and scope of each book.

Books in the Acceptance and Commitment Therapy Series:

- Have an adequate database, appropriate to the strength of the claims being made.

- Are theoretically coherent. They will fit with the ACT model and underlying behavioral principles as they have evolved at the time of writing.

- Orient the reader toward unresolved empirical issues.

- Do not overlap needlessly with existing volumes.

- Avoid jargon and unnecessary entanglement with proprietary methods, leaving ACT work open and available.

- Keep the focus always on what is good for the reader.

- Support the further development of the field.

- Provide information in a way that is of practical use to readers.

These guidelines reflect the values of the broader ACT community. You'll see all of them packed into this book. This series is meant to offer professionals information that can truly be helpful, and to further our ability to alleviate human suffering by inviting creative practitioners into the process of developing, applying, and refining a better approach. This book provides another such invitation.

Sincerely,

Steven C. Hayes, Ph.D., Georg H. Eifert, Ph.D., John Forsyth, Ph.D., and Robyn Walser, Ph.D.

Finding Hope

If you think about life as a series of shifts, there are some that seem to be common to people's experience, regardless of who they are, where they come from, or what they're working toward. For one, at certain times in our lives, we find ourselves stuck. We run up against something difficult—failure, mistreatment, loss, trauma—and it stays with us. It creeps into our thoughts and grabs our attention. Without even realizing it's happening, we start to see our world differently. It seems more threatening, emptier. Without ever choosing to do so, we start to live our lives differently: we make them smaller, safer, more rigid. And one day we look around and notice that we're struggling way too hard and somehow not moving toward anything that really matters to us. We find ourselves stuck, often with no idea how to break free.

There are other moments in our lives when we give up the struggle. We let that sense of how stuck we've become fill us up. We go still. Truly extraordinary things can happen in those moments when we give ourselves permission to be where we are, even if only for a moment. Often it's only by letting ourselves really be stuck that we're able to see the possibility of breaking free.

This book is about the way you've become stuck in certain patterns of eating and about how you can break free. Let's start by considering where you find yourself right now.

LOOKING KINDLY AT YOUR STRUGGLE

Let's assume that you aren't reading this book by accident. If you've taken a look at the cover, you know it's not the kind of book you'd choose to pass the time while waiting for a plane. Chances are you bought this book, picked it up, or were given it because one of the places you get stuck is in your relationship with eating and the way you experience your body. Maybe a doctor has told you that you "have" bulimia nervosa. Maybe someone's referred to you as "a bulimic." Maybe you've just noticed that the people around you don't seem to agonize over their weight or their food like you do. Maybe you've tried to get over these problems, to just stop thinking about how you look or what you eat, and eat like a "normal person." Maybe you've got a sense that you'd better get over these struggles pretty soon—or else.

If the book in your hand were a typical psychology self-help book, we'd start by describing the symptoms of bulimia. We'd explain how it's different from "normal" eating and guess at how it got that way. After that, we'd tell you about different skills you could learn and practice to manage your eating better. We might advise eating moderate portions at regular intervals and give you tips on how to manage urges to overeat. We might instruct you to use relaxation exercises or self-talk or affirmations to relieve some of the stress you've been carrying. We'd offer this to try or that to try, all with the intention of helping you solve your problem with eating.

We feel that we should warn you now: This is not that book. As we go, we'll tell you a little about what mental health providers mean when they say "bulimia." And we'll tell you a little about how we think people get stuck. But when we get to the part on what to do about it, we're going to take you in a new and, we hope, better direction.

You see, most books and most doctors—most people for that matter—approach this struggle called "bulimia" as a problem that needs solving. The thing is, in our experience, solving problems is hard work, and it only works when the thing that's got you stuck actually is a problem.

"Of course it's a problem!" you might be thinking, "What else could it be?" It feels like a problem to you. It looks like one to the people around you. It sure hurts like a problem. But is bulimia a problem to be solved? The truth is, we don't know. We can't know for sure.

We would ask you this, however: Have you spent time figuring out how to quit fighting with your body? Maybe a lot of time? Have you put energy toward finding the perfect solution to your problem with eating? Maybe you've struggled to eat just enough without eating too much. Maybe you've tried to hurry up and lose enough weight so you could finally let go of this struggle. Maybe it feels like if you just struggled a little longer or a little harder or had a little more willpower, a little more time, or a better diet, you could win this battle against your body.

Take a minute right in this moment to draw a long, deep breath and let the ways you've struggled rise up inside you. We're serious. Just stop reading and breathe for a moment. Make room for whatever comes up. Don't judge it; don't try to push it back down or away. Hold whatever happens lightly and with kindness.

Are you tired of this struggle? What has it cost you? What will you have to lose in order to let this go? Maybe you picked up this book because you think you have an eating problem that needs solving. Maybe you're hoping that buried in chapter 7 will be the one solution you've yet to think of. We invite you to think again about what this book might offer—this time, a little differently.

EXERCISE: MATH PROBLEMS AND SUNSETS

At this point, you might be a little confused, and that's okay. We're betting that we can serve you better by taking you someplace new than by telling you things you may have heard before. And we'll do our best to explain where we're coming from. But before we get caught up in explaining, let's spend a little time with an exercise below.

(A note on the exercises in this book: If you are reading this book on an electronic device, it's more than fine to do any of the exercises we offer in an ordinary notebook. If you like, you can also download versions of the longer worksheets at http://20145.nhpubs.com.)

PART 1

▪ Start by finding a pen or pencil. In this exercise, all you need to do is consider what's in the column on the left. Then, in the blank on the right, just write whatever comes to you. These aren't trick questions, we promise. It's not a quiz either. Feel free to use a calculator if you want. Get help if you need it. Just go through the exercise and do what comes naturally.

$2 + 3 =$ _____

$15 - 5 =$ _____

$36 \div 6 =$ _____

$5 \times 5 =$ _____

$6 + 8 =$ _____

$47 - 15 =$ _____

$64 \div 4 =$ _____

$347 \times 19 =$ _____

PART 2

■ The directions for this part are exactly the same as for the first one. Just consider what is on the left. Then, with the blank on the right, just do whatever comes to you.

= _____

So what was that all about?

Well, what was on the left in part 1? In part 1, we gave you math problems. And what occurred to you to do? Most people don't think much about it. Maybe you didn't bother picking up a pen, even as you started through the exercise. You saw "2 + 3" and without even thinking about it, you thought or wrote "5" and moved on to the next one. Maybe you carefully wrote out "5" in the blank in a dark and lovely script. Maybe you grabbed a calculator, just to check your work. Or maybe you took one look at the numbers and the blanks glaring at you and thought, "Not a chance." Whatever form it took, when we gave you a math problem, chances are that you did, or thought about doing, what most people do with a math problem—solve it. One by one, each problem was dealt with, handled, crossed off the list, never to be messed with again. And then you moved on.

All day, every day, you're faced with problem after problem, demanding to be solved. You're just waking up, and you've got class in twenty minutes. The cashier rings up all your purchases and you can't find your wallet. Your phone is ringing from somewhere at the bottom of your bag. Your friend is really hurting, and you don't know how to help her. Your car has splashed into a lake, and it's filling up with water. Looking for and solving problems is most of what you do. It's most of what we all do.

And it's a good thing, too, especially if your wallet is missing. Even more especially if your car is filling up with water. Solving that one quickly and moving on makes a real difference in your life. But problem solving isn't always the most useful approach. Some of the things we face just don't act like problems, although they might be just as distressing. And this is where the second part of the exercise comes in.

What was on the left in part 2? In part 2, we gave you a sunset. So what did you do with it? Better yet, what would you do if we could sit you down and have you look at a real sunset? If you could just open your eyes and there, in front of you, was the sun setting in the west, the ocean on fire, and the sky a dazzling palette of orange, pink, and violet?

Would you solve it? Would you draw on your knowledge of physics to explain what causes that explosion of color in the sky? Would you get out a timetable of sunsets to figure out why, exactly, this happened when it did? Would you try to reason about why the ocean was the way it was? The palm tree? The clouds?

We're guessing you wouldn't. It's pretty obvious that sunsets are different, somehow, from math problems. They don't need solving. They don't need anything. And if you're kind enough to yourself to spend some time with one, the only thing there really is to *do* about a sunset is simply stand there, under a sky ablaze, and soak it all in.

Math Problems, Sunsets, and You

So what happens when the thing you're grappling with is the pain you feel when you look in the mirror? Maybe you've tried to solve that problem by rushing, or searching, or apologizing, or comforting, or escaping. How has that worked for you? What have you tried to do in order to take that pain away for good? Is it the case that you've looked in the mirror and seen a problem, a big problem with your name on it?

When you first saw this "problem," you probably did what humans typically do with problems. You probably worked harder; you tried to figure it all out, to get a grip on things. In other words, you tried to solve the problem of yourself, just like you did with those math problems. And in the process, you might have started to feel as if you were digging yourself in a little deeper, as if you were more and more stuck all the time.

But what if your experience of yourself wasn't like a math problem? What if trying to solve the "problem" of yourself makes little more sense than trying to solve a sunset? What if they just don't need solving? What if *you* don't need solving? What if all this time, you've been fighting these urges, these fears, these doubts, this pain, as if they were math problems, when all along they were just things about you, like sunsets, that could be seen and appreciated without being fixed, solved, or gotten rid of? What if, in a world of problems to be solved, *you* are a sunset? What if standing back and taking in the experiences that rise up inside could help you find the freedom to live a richer, fuller life of your design without anything having to be solved first?

If you're not convinced that this might be possible, good. We don't want to convince you. At this point, all we want you to do is let an idea well up inside you: that you *might* not need to solve your "problem" with eating before you can get to the business of living your life. See what it *might* feel like. There's nothing wrong with being skeptical.

Let's look at this a little more closely. Imagine this book was that book that it isn't—that book that was all about solving your problems. Imagine that you did every exercise perfectly and learned every skill the book had to teach. Imagine that the skills you learned from this book worked really, really well.

Imagine that by putting these skills into practice, you were able to rid yourself once and for all of the fear and frustration and regret and self-doubt that have had you stuck. Imagine you were able to work hard enough to get rid of your distress about eating and your body. Imagine setting down your pencil upon finishing the last page of the book, closing the cover—and finding that your problems with eating and body images were just gone.

Well. Now what are you going to do?

Seriously. Where do you go? How do you move about your world? You don't have to write anything down just yet or tell anybody an answer. In fact, hesitate here a minute, just beyond the question, but just outside of the answer. Let that question sort of resonate.

If you managed to solve your problems perfectly, the question posed by the book you're actually holding would still remain—and the answer you come up with for this question can be nothing short of your very life. And we think that your time and energy are much better spent answering this great question than they would be in trying to figure out the solution to all of the problems you're going to face from now on. Maybe you can find the perfect solution to your struggle. Maybe you can't. But maybe there's another option. Maybe you can live your life richly and purposefully without getting rid of or solving any problem. Maybe living the answer to this great question doesn't have to wait for anything. Maybe you can start living right now.

SOMETHING COMPLETELY DIFFERENT

It's probably obvious, but we firmly believe that you can, indeed, start living a meaningful and sincere life without getting rid of bulimia first. This book is our attempt to offer you a means to do it.

We're basing this means on a kind of psychotherapy called *acceptance and commitment therapy*, or "ACT" (said as the word, "act," rather than the letters) for short. ACT offers an approach to living a rich life with the kinds of experiences we often call "problems," experiences that, when we try to solve them like problems, often leave us stuck.

ACT was developed based on the idea that experiences like the ones we often call eating disorders, anxiety disorders, or mood disorders emerge when we try to fix our experiences of ourselves and the world. ACT isn't popular or inspirational psychology. It grew out of a tradition in behavioral science called *behavior analysis*. As you read this, ACT is being refined and tested in studies around the world, and psychologists are discovering new ways to make use of it. Since its development, ACT has been effectively applied to not only the difficulties we call "disorders" but also issues like physical pain and disability, stress and burnout, and prejudice and discrimination.

The Purpose

ACT breaks significantly from many other kinds of therapy by not focusing on getting rid of or reducing the symptoms of particular mental health disorders. We've spent some time so far hinting that you might be better off letting go of problem solving rather than chasing some kind of new solution. This idea is consistent with ACT as a therapy. ACT isn't about making symptoms of eating disorders, anxiety disorders, or mood disorders go away. Regardless of the name you might choose to give it, ACT is about letting go of whatever you're struggling with so you can start building a richer and more meaningful life. That richer, more meaningful life is the ultimate purpose of ACT—and we sometimes call this purpose *valued living*.

"Okay," you might be thinking, "that all sounds great and everything, but how exactly is that going to happen? How am I going to go from where I am now to a 'richer, more meaningful life'?"

If you feel that thought or another like it rising up and the world squeezing down as doubt and anxiety overcome you—stop. Now take a deep, long, slow breath. And as you exhale, notice how easy it was for you to lurch into problem solving. It may not have even been clear to you what the problems were that might be obstacles between you and a richer, more meaningful life—or even that there were such problems. But your mind did what minds do: you started working on a "solution." ACT isn't about solving the problem of bulimia, or the problem with you, *or* the problem of a meaningless life. ACT is about *living* that meaningful life. Fortunately, we've already started to hint at how that can happen.

The Goal

ACT takes a new and different perspective on psychological health. It's not focused on solving all problems or even on being particularly good at problem solving. From an ACT perspective, psychological health involves opening up to your experiences in such a way that you get to take steps toward the things you care about, even when fear or frustration or regret is present. The idea is to become fully aware of the experiences that get you stuck, to practice letting go of attempts to change them, shifting the focus of your actions to the things that matter to you. In ACT this is called *psychological flexibility*, and it's just the opposite of being stuck in your struggle.

Notice the difference between the purpose (valued living) and the goal (psychological flexibility). In ACT, there's this idea that even psychological health is not for nothing. Being flexible is not particularly virtuous in and of itself. The only reason flexibility matters is because being open to difficult experiences means you get to keep moving through and around those experiences, no matter what kind of thoughts, feelings, or emotions show up. Being able to keep moving means being able to keep doing the things that matter to you. In other words, psychological flexibility is important only to the extent that it allows for valued living. In the same way, the skills we present in this book matter only to the extent that they allow for *your* valued living.

WHAT YOU CAN EXPECT FROM THIS BOOK

If any of this is sounding strange or confusing, good. That means you're paying attention. You're paying attention well enough to notice that this approach is different—not just different from most therapies or self-help books but different from most people's general outlook. This is not how we've been taught to look at the world—and certainly not how we've been taught to look at our own pain. One thing you can expect from this book is that there will be times when this perspective and this work feel really off to you. There will be times when you feel really confused. This is a side effect of taking a completely different orientation on the world than that you've been walking around with, probably for your whole life. Like driving or walking in a new city for the first time, this can be disorienting for a while.

As you can probably guess, we don't have a handy remedy for this confusion. Getting around in a strange place is disorienting even when it allows you to see new and exciting things. Playing with this new perspective is disorienting even when it allows you to see your life—your pain and your values— more clearly.

So when confusion threatens your moving forward in this book, when you think, "This is just too confusing to be helpful," call to mind the things you really care about. Go ahead and do it now.

Take a minute and call to mind something that really matters to you, something you care about deeply but don't always feel you're the best at working on. Don't skip ahead here. Stop reading long enough to draw a full breath and visualize that person or idea you care about. Now ask yourself if it is worth being confused if there's a possibility that this work could move you toward that something that really matters to you. You don't have to answer right away. Just let the question linger for a while.

You've probably noticed that we keep telling you to stop and breathe to consider this or that while drawing a couple of full breaths. We're big advocates of breathing, of noticing breathing. Everybody breathes, but not too many of us take the time to notice that we are doing it. When things get hectic in your head, taking a moment to stop and notice your breath can be a powerful exercise. Stopping to breathe with awareness and intention when you just want to get moving far away from whatever is going on for you can be a little mini-practice in that flexibility stuff we were talking about. Notice what's here, let go of struggling with it, and move forward with intention. Sometimes the next right step toward valued living is just to let ourselves fall still for a moment and to draw that next breath. So we're going to drop in instructions like that even in the middle of explanations of this idea or that. And if you get anything out of those quiet moments, we'll ask you to go ahead and add some of your own, while you're doing the work here in this book and while you're living life out there in the world.

Breathing isn't the only thing we'll ask you to do. We'll be the first to admit that merely reading this text, even reading it carefully without skipping a word, is not likely to have a noticeable or long-term effect on your life. You've been practicing getting stuck for years now. Probably not always with eating, but with all kinds of struggles. Ten, fifteen, thirty years you may have spent practicing getting stuck, learning more and more things about yourself and the world to get stuck around. And you could read the words in this book in a week or two. Mere reading isn't likely to make the kinds of changes in your life we are hoping for. We don't offer this book to *tell you about* seeing and doing differently. We offer this book as an opportunity to see and do differently.

Folks have started to do the research to see who really benefits from books like this, and they're finding that it's those readers who actually try the things they read about. So breathing isn't the only mini-practice we're going to introduce. This book is going to have parts that tell you about a perspective, but the more important parts are going to be the parts that ask you to experience that perspective. This book is going to have parts that tell you about a skill, but the more important parts are going to be the parts that ask you to practice that skill. And, regardless of our great explanation of why this is important, don't do any of this because we asked you to. Remember, our purpose here is *your* valued living. See if you can't really engage in these exercises, not for the sake of doing what you're told or what makes sense, but for the possibility that this could be the next step in living the life that matters to you.

WHO WE ARE

As we will ask you about your life, and ask you to consider the things that matter the most and hurt the most, it makes sense to us to tell you a little more about ourselves. Kelly is a professor in the Department of Psychology at the University of Mississippi. A coauthor of the 1999 book *Acceptance and Commitment Therapy*, he has been one of the people largely responsible for developing and helping to shape ACT into what it is today. He's a popular trainer and speaker, traveling often to engage with people about ACT and behavior analysis. He has a fondness for coffee, guitars, Apple products, and the tropical parts of Mexico—the latter especially when he gets to swim in warm ocean water with his wife and his daughters.

Emily worked with Kelly when she was completing her Ph.D. in psychology at Ole Miss. She is now a professor in the Department of Psychology at the University of Louisiana at Lafayette. In her time at Ole Miss, Emily wrote, provided therapy, and provided professional training under Kelly's supervision. She also began a program of research on body image and disordered eating that she is continuing to build now that she's out on her own. Emily has crazy ideas about making the world a better place for her kids, the virtues of dancing like nobody's looking, and the essentials of a good margarita. And she will talk about them to just about anyone.

Troy is a writer who, mostly by chance, has become a fellow traveler with the folks in the ACT community. He started writing psychology and self-help books in 2006 with a book titled *Coping with OCD*. In 2007, Troy stumbled into an ACT workshop Kelly was conducting in Houston, Texas. Troy actually didn't want to go to that particular workshop, but his first choice was full. So there he was. Emily was assisting at that workshop, and she partnered with Troy in several of the experiential exercises. Troy's chance meeting with Kelly eventually resulted in their 2008 collaboration on the book *Mindfulness for Two*, which is a book specifically about present-moment-contact issues in psychotherapy. As Kelly's student, Emily tagged along for the ride, offering some writing and role-playing along the way. After that, Kelly and Troy worked together on a book about anxiety for general readers called *Things Might Go Terribly, Horribly Wrong*. And at another conference in Chicago, the three of us started talking about this book—and its professionally focused cousin, *Acceptance and Commitment Therapy for Eating Disorders*.

Those little details of where we've been and where we find ourselves are one way of telling you about us. And each of them is perfectly true. Another way would be equally true: We are people who, at one time or another, have found ourselves stuck. The conversations in Chicago that resulted in our writing this book were not about how horribly *other* people struggle and how we just don't understand how they get there. They were about the pain *we* struggle with and the pain our struggles cause *us*. We are people who have known the struggle and who have known letting go of the struggle. And we think there's something precious that comes from letting go.

The details of *your* life we don't know. Where you live, how old you are, what you do for fun. In some ways, this makes it harder for us to write the book that would be most useful to you. If we had to guess, though (and we do), we'd guess that you are not all that different from us: That you have found yourself stuck. That you've known the pain *you* struggle with and the pain that struggle causes *you*. That, in particular, the way you eat and don't eat and struggle with eating is just not doing it for you anymore.

COME AS YOU ARE: AN INVITATION

And so we'd like to offer you an invitation. It's not like an invitation to a party, where we are already there enjoying the beverages and entertainment. It's like an invitation to accompany us on a journey. And this journey is pretty unique. We're not sure exactly where it's going to take us. We are guided by a few ideas that are more mission goals than directions—more like "find a leaf of the red oak tree" than "walk thirteen paces due south." And what's really extraordinary about this journey is not where we find ourselves at the end of it, but how we find ourselves moving along the way. You don't want to miss anything, so you move slowly, taking it all in. Our wish is that the time you spend with this book will be time in which you can rest. We don't know what will happen a year, five years, ten years from now, but there will be time enough to get there. The journey we are inviting you to is one that is as long or as brief as you want it to be. You might decide to part ways with us today and chuck this book into the garbage can on your way out the door. You might find yourself taking the ideas we present and leading yourself places you've never gone and maybe never thought you could find your way to. This could be the first day of your life's journey.

So when you're ready, let's get started. Know that we feel sincerely honored by your company through these pages.

CHAPTER 1

Some Things You Should Know About How We Eat and How We See Ourselves

As you've probably noticed, the struggle we've talked about in this book isn't just disordered eating. Some folks struggle by pulling the covers up over their heads, some folks struggle by limiting the places they go, and some folks struggle by eating a certain way. So there will be times when the things we ask you to think about or try out are really general and would apply to most people. There are other times when we focus on the topic of this book—a struggle some folks call "bulimia."

WHAT IS "BULIMIA"?

You might be thinking it's a little strange for us to have quotation marks around a diagnosis. The doctor doesn't sit you down in his office to tell you that you have "cancer." He tells you the name, then he tells you what your body is doing that's causing you problems. Psychological problems are a little different, though. When we say "psychology," we're referring to the science of behavior. (Just to be clear: this isn't exactly what everyone means when they say "psychology." But we come from a tradition of behavioral science, and when we say "psychology," that's what we mean specifically.) Behavior is anything a person does. People come into therapy because they keep doing things that are causing them problems. Whether the behavior that brings them in consists of the way they're feeling, the way they're thinking, or the actions they're taking, something they're doing just isn't working. Our diagnoses don't *explain* what's going on underneath the problems people show up with, they simply *describe* what those problematic behaviors look like.

What Bulimia Looks Like

"Bulimia" (or "bulimia nervosa") is a name for a particular category of problematic behaviors. When doctors and other providers say "bulimia," they're referring to three main behaviors: binge eating, compensatory behaviors, and body image difficulties. Now, you might have some idea of what each of these means (or you might be thinking, "What language is this?"), but we're going to go ahead and describe what these terms mean to the providers who use them.

BINGE EATING

The first term, "binge eating," means eating more food than most people would eat in a similar situation, along with a feeling that you lack control over this eating. This is from the current technical definition. Many have noted, however, that it doesn't seem to be the amount of food that's important. A "binge" might be better defined as any time you eat what, for you, seems like an abnormal amount of food. If you have a very rigid diet and rarely eat meats, dairy, or white bread, then eating three pieces of pepperoni pizza might be as much of a "binge" as three whole pizzas for the person who eats pizza regularly. Psychologists who do research on how bulimia looks and how we should best think about these categories have suggested that the more important part may be the lack of control that comes with a binge. It may not matter if it's three bites of pizza, three slices, or three whole pies. If it feels like you ate way more than you intended, it may be accurate to call it a "binge."

PRACTICE: REFLECTING ON BINGE EATING (GUIDED MEDITATION)

We invite you to pause for a moment now and consider what "binge eating" looks like for you. We don't expect this to be easy, but we do ask you not to rush through this practice or skip to the next piece. We often do whatever we can to push difficult things like this out of our minds. We hide our behaviors from others, and we try to forget that they happen. This is part of what keeps us stuck.

You can read through the instructions to this practice first, get a feel for them, then set the book down to do the work. Or you can do the practice along with the first guided meditation on the CD (or the download, if you bought the e-book), titled "Reflecting on Bulimia." *Note:* The audio that accompanies this book was recorded spontaneously, and although it is similar to the text in the book, it doesn't follow the text exactly, so you may not want to read and listen at the same time.

■ Take a slow, deep breath. Close your eyes, and call to mind a specific time when you felt a real lack of control over your eating. Maybe you were completely unaware of what was going on while you were eating, then suddenly realized that you'd eaten way more than you intended. Call up this memory from the moment just before you started to eat, and watch yourself. See if you can stay with the memory long enough to let that experience rise up fully inside you. And breathe.

■ When you find yourself turning away from you and your experience, take a slow, deep breath and turn back. When you find yourself rushing through the memory, trying to get it over with, take a slow, deep breath and turn back to the beginning. Don't you deserve to be seen, even in your weakest moments?

■ When you've settled into this specific memory, let yourself consider your pattern of "binge eating" over time. Are there certain "forbidden" foods you tend to binge on? Are there certain situations in which you tend to binge eat? Do you tend to binge eat in a certain place? During certain times of day? Are you more likely to binge eat after a certain kind of experience? When you're feeling a certain way? What is it like for you during a binge? After?

■ Take a moment now and let yourself see clearly the details that seem important about what is going on for you before, during, and after a binge. And breathe.

■ When you're ready, let your eyes slowly open.

If you're using the paper book, take a few moments and write about your reflections in the space below. If you're using an electronic version of the book, do the same thing in a notebook or journal.

What "binge eating" looks like for me: _____

_____

_____

_____

We'd like to take a moment here and acknowledge how difficult recalling the details of these experiences can be. If you took the time and energy to do this, we applaud you. Sitting with these difficult experiences will serve you well in this work. If you left the lines above blank, we encourage you to just notice how hard it is to even think about this. Yet here you are, seeking help. Now we invite you to take a slow, deep breath and let those difficult thoughts and feelings pass gently as we turn to the next thing.

COMPENSATORY BEHAVIOR

The second term in our definition of bulimia, "compensatory behavior," means repeatedly responding to binges by doing things to avoid weight gain. This doesn't mean just eating less next time that situation comes up; it means doing something specifically to compensate for the way you ate before. Many people associate bulimia with vomiting, but this is just one example of compensatory behavior. Some people take laxatives, exercise excessively, starve themselves, or use diet pills.

As in the last section, we invite you to take a moment to reflect on what "compensatory behaviors" might mean for you.

PRACTICE: REFLECTING ON COMPENSATORY BEHAVIORS (GUIDED MEDITATION)

- Call to mind the things that you might do to make up for your binge eating. Take a slow, deep breath. Close your eyes, and call to mind a specific time when you reacted to a binge in this way.

- Call up this memory from the moment your binge ended, and watch yourself move into trying to make up for it. See if you can stay with the memory long enough to let that experience rise up fully inside you. And breathe.

- When you find yourself turning away from you and your experience, take a slow, deep breath and turn back. When you find yourself rushing through the memory, trying to get it over with, take a slow, deep breath and turn back to the beginning. And we ask you once more—don't you deserve to be seen, even in your weakest moments?

- When you've settled into this specific memory, let yourself consider your pattern of "compensatory behavior" over time. What are the different ways that you make up for binge eating? Are there certain situations in which you tend to react in this way? Certain times of day? How do you typically feel as you carry this out? After?

- When you're ready, allow your eyes to gently open.

If you're willing at this moment, write down below or in your notebook the details of what is going on for you before, during, and after your compensatory behavior.

What "compensatory behavior" looks like for me: _____

_____

_____

_____

Again, if you took the time and energy to do this, we applaud you. This is not easy work, but you'll find that everything we do will build on these small, brief practices. We invite you to take a deep breath and let any difficult thoughts and feelings that you are hanging on to pass gently as we turn to the next thing.

BODY IMAGE DIFFICULTY

Binge eating and compensatory behavior often come with what we call "body image difficulties." This makes a lot of sense. How you feel about your body can have a large effect on how you feel about yourself. If you're feeling thin, you may feel good about yourself—confident and secure. If you're feeling fat, you may feel bad about yourself—unsure and insecure. Because weight and body shape can change quickly when your eating is imbalanced, this often can mean that your feelings about yourself change often and quickly. One minute you're feeling great about yourself, like you're beautiful and competent, but the moment you feel bloated or catch a glimpse of a certain part of your body, you suddenly feel ugly and like everything could fall apart at any time. Some research has suggested that this instability of feelings about yourself is even more harmful than feeling bad about yourself most of the time (Melnyk, Cash, and Janda 2004).

Now let's take a few moments to consider how body image is working in your life.

PRACTICE: REFLECTING ON BODY IMAGE (GUIDED MEDITATION)

- Let your eyes gently close, and just notice your own "body image." When do you feel good about your body? You may feel good about your body when your mood is good or when other things are going right.

- What do you see in the moments you see your body as "good"? Maybe you focus on seeing the bones in your hips or seeing your clothes hang in a certain way. What do you feel in your body in the moments you feel your body is "good"? Maybe you focus on tightness in your muscles or your stomach. Take a moment here and write down the things you're seeing, feeling, or otherwise experiencing when you feel good about your body.

- When do you feel bad about your body? For example, some people notice they feel bad about their bodies when their mood is bad or when other things are going wrong. What do you see in the moments you see your body as "fat" or "ugly"? You may focus on seeing your stomach stick out or seeing your clothes pull in a certain way.

■ What do you feel in your body in the moments you feel your body is "fat" or "ugly"? Some people tend to focus on a full feeling in their stomachs. And breathe.

■ Pause here and notice the role that your body image has in your life. What else do you feel when you feel bad about your body? What kind of thoughts come up for you? How do you see yourself as a person when you're feeling bad about your body? What else do you do differently?

■ When you're ready, allow your eyes to gently open.

Now, if you're willing, take a few moments to record what came up for you in the practice by writing in the spaces below or in your notebook.

When I feel good about my body, I feel: _____

_____

_____

_____

When I feel good about my body, I think: _____

_____

_____

_____

When I feel good about my body, I see myself as: _____

_____

_____

_____

When I feel good about my body, I tend to: _____

_____

_____

_____

When I feel bad about my body, I feel: _____

_____

_____

_____

When I feel bad about my body, I think: _____

_____

_____

_____

When I feel bad about my body, I see myself as: _____

_____

_____

_____

When I feel bad about my body, I tend to: _____

_____

_____

_____

Now, we invite you to take three slow, deep breaths before moving on. These are simple questions we are asking, but they're not easy.

About Categories

Now let's talk some more about definitions. When folks say "bulimia" (if they know what they're talking about), they're talking about a pattern of binge eating, then trying to make up for binge eating, along with a self-image that's based mostly on the body. When this occurs in a person's life at least twice a week for three months and gets in the way of her life, if the person is not underweight, she can be diagnosed with "bulimia nervosa." If she is underweight, she can be diagnosed with "anorexia nervosa." (Anorexia has its own description, but quite a bit of that description overlaps with bulimia.) If the behavior described has occurred less often or for a shorter amount of time, or if the person more often binges without compensating, she can be diagnosed with "eating disorder, not otherwise specified," which is abbreviated as EDNOS.

We'd like to stop and notice here that there are lots of categories to get lost in. Yet, all these categories do is communicate what a person is doing that's causing problems. In fact, if it isn't causing problems in the person's life, it isn't diagnosed.

At this point, you might be scrambling to figure out which of these categories best fits your situation. You might be puzzling about whether your behavior should be called "bulimia," "anorexia," "EDNOS," or something else altogether. You might find yourself considering, "But is it really causing me *problems*? I mean, what do they mean by *problems*?" It might feel really important to put a name on your struggle, or to compare what's described here with what you may have heard before picking up this book. It might feel like a relief to have a name for your struggle or to find your struggle doesn't quite match any of these. On the other hand, those discoveries might feel disappointing to you.

Whatever is going on for you in this moment, we ask you to briefly stop reading and let your experience rise up inside of you. Take a couple of long, deep breaths and notice any thoughts or feelings that are there. And as you breathe, see if you can't open yourself up to whatever is going on there, for you, right now. And whenever you're ready, we ask you to gently let go of any efforts you're making to figure this out or make it fit your situation. Take one last breath, and move on to the next thing.

No matter what category your behavior fits in, if you find yourself stuck in a pattern of eating more than you intended, trying to make up for that in ways that harm you, and letting your feelings about your body determine your feelings about yourself, then there may be things you could learn from this book. So we invite you to settle in and stay awhile.

Oh, and another thing to note about diagnostic categories: the ways doctors and psychologists think about categories like "bulimia" isn't fixed or permanent. The understanding of these categories changes over time. As we write this, in 2010, the American Psychiatric Association is busy working on a new set of diagnostic criteria for mental health problems. These new guidelines will be published in the fifth edition of the *Diagnostic and Statistical Manual of Mental Disorders*, scheduled to be released in 2013. The diagnostic criteria for eating disorders, in particular, are likely to change in this new edition. What do you think? On the first morning the *DSM-V* is available, do you think you'll feel very different about your relationship with food and the way you look? If not, maybe there's more to this struggle than the labels you can put on how it looks.

What Bulimia Costs

More important than what bulimia looks like is what bulimia costs. It doesn't matter so much whether you're bingeing without compensating, or compensating without a true binge, or just exercising like crazy every time you overeat. It's not important if you've been struggling with it for six weeks or more like six years. What really matters most is how your life has started to bend around this struggle, how many things that matter to you you've given up because of the way you relate to food, how much bulimic behaviors have cost you.

COSTS IN YOUR BODY

The first and most obvious costs you're likely to recognize are the physical ones. Physicians and other medical professionals don't have the least bit of doubt that bulimic behaviors take a serious toll on your body. Binge eating can stretch out the stomach or even cause it to rupture. Purging with laxatives or by vomiting can cause dehydration and a serious electrolyte imbalance, putting you at risk for a heart attack. Excessive exercise weakens your immune system and can destroy your muscles, especially if you're also purging. The list goes on and on.

The body just isn't made to handle this kind of repeated physical stress. Maybe you've found yourself becoming weaker and weaker. Maybe you've started to struggle to catch your breath a little more often. Maybe you've felt your heart beating irregularly, like it was fighting to get its rhythm back. Maybe your muscles hurt all the time or you've noticed your teeth, your skin, and your hair aren't looking quite as healthy as they used to. Take a moment here and write down, below or in your notebook, any physical changes you've noticed in your body:

_____

_____

_____

COSTS IN YOUR LIFE

This struggle doesn't just have costs in your body. Eating difficulties like this tend to gradually take up more and more of your life until it's hard to give energy to anything else. People describe having never really intended to give things up for good, but that somehow, over time, they found their lives getting smaller and smaller.

Maybe you find yourself avoiding more and more parties, dinners, or other social events. Maybe you've begun to let go of relationships that used to feel important to you. Maybe you've fallen behind at work or in class. Maybe you can call to mind a time when you used to really like to sing, or write, or watch movies, or play volleyball. Maybe you find yourself less and less present more and more often.

As a gift to yourself, we invite you to take a look at your life and see what things you've let go of to keep both hands in this struggle. Offer yourself a couple of slow, deep breaths. Then, call to mind a time in your life when you were moving more freely than you are now. Without forming an answer, just notice the life you built every day, a little at a time: the places you went, the things you did. How has your movement about your life changed? What might you be doing if you didn't have both hands tied up in this struggle?

You might find this hard to read without thinking something like, "Surely it's not that bad... I still work out, and I make the same grades as ever..." If you find yourself reaching for reasons, explanations, or justifications, if you find yourself working to dismiss the costs of your struggle with your body and eating, it may be useful to spend just a little more time lingering in the questions. Is there a cost here that matters enough to you to continue with this work? Is there a missing piece of your life that you'd be willing to work to get back? We invite you to write down any examples of ways bulimia has cost you:

_____

_____

_____

When you've given yourself some time with these questions, we invite you to take a moment to consider another question. If you were to wake one morning and this struggle with bulimia had suddenly fallen away, what is the first thing you would do? Linger for a moment in the question, then go ahead and settle upon an answer. Write that answer down below or in your notebook. It will likely be useful on our journey.

If I were to suddenly find my struggle with food and my body had fallen away, I would: _____

_____

_____

_____

HOW WE LEARN TO GET STUCK IN THINGS THAT HURT US

We've all watched people we care about do things over and over that obviously hurt them, that obviously leave them stuck. One gets drunk or high every time things get hard. Another puts things off until it's way too late to do the job right. Still another settles for less than he wants and deserves. This one keeps returning to rotten relationships that slowly beat her down. That one never tries his best at anything that matters to him. Another spends money she doesn't have on things she doesn't need. Let yourself notice how often this has come up in your life in one form or another.

PRACTICE: SITTING WITH SUFFERING

Take a deep, slow breath and call to mind a specific time when you watched someone you care about do that same, familiar thing that just earns him or her more trouble and pain. Write that person's name here or in your notebook: _____

Now consider the thing he or she does. If there are several ways that person hurts herself or himself, let yourself settle upon one. Write down a few words describing what that person does that hurts him or her:

_____

_____

_____

Now imagine that one day next week, you find yourself with this person you care about, watching as they make moves you know are going to hurt them. If you're willing, close your eyes and let that specific image rise up, along with any thoughts or feelings it brings with it. There she is, just asking for more pain. There he is, just digging himself deeper and deeper in. Watch yourself as this occurs, paying special attention to your reaction. What kind of thoughts are running through your head? How do you feel about this person? About this situation? What do you do? How do you handle this? Write down a few words here describing what you notice about your reaction in this exercise: _____

_____

_____

_____

For most of us, there's some degree of pain, frustration, guilt, or disappointment that comes with watching people we care about hurt themselves. We might find ourselves wondering how they could do this *again*. We might find ourselves racking our brains as to what we could do to *make them stop*. Often, when faced with a situation like this, we do two things.

First, we do whatever we think might work to stop the person. We try to explain the consequences we've noticed. We try to convince them to do something different. We tell them what we would do. We might even try to force them to do what seems right. We might threaten to leave if something doesn't change. Often, after doing what we can to stop them, the only thing we can see left to do is turn away. Sometimes we literally remove ourselves from the situation. We make an excuse to get off the phone. We leave the room and engage ourselves in something else. We avoid the person for a while, wait for things to settle down a little. Sometimes our turn away is less obvious. We just sort of disengage, staying polite but not connected. Or we just don't talk about the obvious, changing the subject when the liquor, or the relationship, or the job comes up. We find a way to push it away. "If they're going to keep hurting themselves, at least I can protect myself."

"Of course!" you might be thinking. "I can't understand how they keep doing this, so what else can I do?" But here's the thing—we don't turn away because we *are not* able to understand what the person we care about is going through. In fact, it may be quite the opposite. Research into how humans relate to one another suggests that we cannot see another's sadness without feeling our own (Hayes 1984; Vilardaga 2009). And, in the same way, we cannot turn away from our own sadness without having to turn away from that of others.

We see others hurting themselves, and we turn away. What if it is not because we can't understand how it is that they could continue to do things that hurt themselves over and over? What if we turn away because we know all too well what they're going through? Maybe it looks different on the outside. Maybe we have different methods and different reasons. But what if we all do things that hurt us and get in our own way? What if that's just what life is like for humans? What if your struggle with your body and food is just one example of the many ways people can learn to hurt themselves?

A NOTE ON LEARNING: IT'S ALL IN THE CONTEXT

This book, like ACT more generally, is based on a very simple idea: that much of what we think, feel, and do is learned through our experiences with the world. From this perspective, thinking, feeling, and doing are all behavior. And behavior is influenced by its *context*, or the events that happen around it, and by our *history*, or how we've experienced those things in the past.

Some context is made up of events that come before the behavior. Maybe you cringe and feel anxious in the context of a screeching sound. From this perspective, we would assume this is because of your history with screeching sounds. Maybe a screeching sound has come before car accidents in your past. Eventually, you've come to react to just the screeching sound by wincing and feeling anxious, even without having a car accident. In the same way, if the smell of a campfire has come before an enjoyable cookout in your past, you're likely to smile and feel excited in the context of a campfire smell, even if you aren't at a cookout. You smile and feel excited in the context of a campfire smell because of your history with campfire smells.

Some context is made of the events that are consequences of the behavior, or the things that happen after you act. Maybe every time you see a crying baby, you pat her on the back. From this perspective, we would assume this is because of your history with crying babies. Maybe patting a crying baby on the back has often stopped its crying. Over time, patting becomes the thing you're most likely to do once a baby starts crying. In the same way, if you put the television on channel 42 and a movie you like comes on, you're more likely to check channel 42 the next time you encounter that television. You're likely to put on channel 42 because of your history with the consequences of putting the TV on channel 42.

If this is how we learn to do the things we do, how is it that humans could be so good at learning to do things that cause them harm? How can people learn to restrict, to binge eat, or to purge, with all the accompanying consequences? How is it that you could have learned to act in a way that has costs to your health, your relationships, or your life in general? In other words, what is the *context* and *history* in which those behaviors would "work"?

Thoughts and Feelings: The Context We Carry with Us

If you consider what we've explained above, it seems that the kinds of behaviors we call bulimia would be almost impossible to learn. Clearly many of the consequences of binge eating, purging, and other compensatory behaviors are horrible. The kinds of costs that result from these behaviors are things that humans would typically work to avoid. Yet, these behaviors are learned.

It turns out that human learning is complicated by the fact that the context we respond to is not made up only of events that occur outside of our skin. Some behaviors are related to the things happening within us. For example, some behaviors are more likely in the context of certain thoughts or feelings. You may be more likely to yell when you feel angry or to sing when you feel happy. You may also be likely to respond to imagined events as if they (and not just thoughts of them) were happening in the moment. Just as you might wince and feel anxious in response to a screeching sound, you might wince and feel anxious as you hear someone describe slamming on the brakes to avoid an accident. And not only that: just as you might pat a baby's back to make crying stop, you might do any number of things to try to make memories, or worry, or painful feelings stop—even if these things actually cause you problems, even if you *know* these things actually cause you problems.

(Now if you are really paying close attention, you might notice that earlier we talked about thoughts and feelings as behavior, and now we are saying they are part of the context. We didn't mess up. That's exactly what we mean. They are behaviors, and they can be the context for other behaviors. Trust us on this one.)

A VICIOUS CYCLE

This is how many of the things we do that hurt us tend to work. Often what keeps us doing them is that instant of relief they bring, even if the long-term consequence of doing them is more suffering. If we look a bit more closely at how bulimic behaviors work, often behind them there are some painful thoughts or feelings being managed. You're hurting, and without even thinking about why, you start to eat. Without knowing how, you get a little bit of distance from the pain you've been carrying. Maybe in your history, you've used food as a reward, a celebration, or a comfort. And just as you gain distance from the painful thoughts and feelings, you're distanced for some time from the experience of eating and feelings of fullness. Until you aren't. And then the pain returns, this time with the physical discomfort of fullness and psychological guilt or shame that comes with it. And maybe in your history, feeling full has meant being selfish, or gluttonous, or bad. So there you are again, seeking relief, this time through compensatory behaviors. So you purge or you starve or you exercise until you get a little bit of relief from that feeling. And that relief lasts as long as it lasts, until the cycle starts again.

Just like patting the baby to stop her crying, each instant of relief makes the behavior it follows more probable in the future, regardless of its long-term consequences. Even worrying about the costs of bulimia can result in more bulimic behaviors, as you seek relief from feeling concerned.

We invite you to take a moment here and look back at your earlier answers where you described your body image and what "binge eating" and "compensatory behaviors" look like for you. If you wrote down what comes before these behaviors and what comes after these behaviors, then you have a head start on considering your eating and body image *in context*. We're not going to ask you to write anything else down just yet, but do take a moment and reread what you wrote, noticing how bulimic behaviors might bring you relief in the short term.

THERE IS NO EASY WAY TO TURN OFF YOUR THOUGHTS

So, if you're engaging in harmful bulimic behaviors in order to manage painful thoughts and feelings, wouldn't it make more sense just to stop and change those thoughts? This sounds like a good idea at first. You've probably tried to do this on some level or another. You've told yourself you're being silly, you've badgered yourself to "let it go," you've reminded yourself of all the good things people say about you. Yet here you are, still stuck and looking for a way out.

Turns out that changing your thinking *is* a good idea on many levels. Some therapy approaches treat bulimia specifically by focusing on trying to change thinking in order to change feelings and behavior. And they work pretty well at helping people stop bulimic behaviors. We're just not sure that they work by actually changing thinking.

For one thing, trying to make thoughts or feelings stop is problematic because events in our thoughts don't work quite the same way as events out in the world. If you encounter an offensive noise, an itchy feeling, or an annoyingly bright light, you can plug your ears, change your sweater, or draw the curtains and—voilà—your problem is solved. And trying to control uncomfortable thoughts and feelings might give you short-term relief. You might successfully push a memory out of your mind, talk yourself out of a fear, or distract yourself from something that's hurting. But before long, efforts like these tend to result in *more* of the very thoughts you were trying to avoid.

The reasons for this are kind of complex, and psychologists are still in the process of working out all the details. To get a sense of why this is so, though, take just a moment and try *not* to think about a horse. Go ahead. Give it a try. Think about whatever you want, as long as it's not a horse.

Now, chances are you weren't thinking about a horse when you read the preceding paragraph for the first time, and you might not even have much reason to think about horses at all. But if you specifically try *not* to think about them, with each effort, you're actually calling them to mind: "Don't think about a HORSE. Don't think about a HORSE." And if it's hard with a totally random thought that doesn't have much to do with your life, imagine how hard it is with something that has been with you and causing you pain for a long time.

Next, we humans are really good at focusing on things that cause us pain or discomfort, particularly if we have ways of getting relief. When things stay difficult for a while, we can easily come to a place where we pay attention only to the things that hurt us and the things that signal hurt. Have you ever had back pain, a toothache, or even a mild sore throat? Do you remember how hard it was to focus on the other things going on in your life? How much did you notice pleasant things like the warm sunshine or the breeze on your face? During this time, did you jump at the chance to connect with someone you care about or pursue an opportunity for growth? Chances are you missed at least some of what was going on in your life because your attention was focused on what was hurting you. This is very natural for humans. We become so focused on managing feelings that the rest of the world, the rest of our lives even, falls away.

Finally, uncomfortable thoughts and feelings often (or, really, always) show up right inside of things that we care about. We feel grief when we've lost a relationship precisely because that relationship mattered to us. We feel frustration when something we really, really want slips out of our reach. We feel anxiety or anger when something comes up that might threaten the things we care about. We feel sadness when we make a mistake that puts us further from the things we want in life. And how do we feel when a trivial relationship falls apart? When we miss the chance to get something that didn't matter all that much to us in the first place? When someone we don't know at all finds himself in a jam?

The point here is that many of the things that tear us apart inside wouldn't matter a bit if there wasn't something we valued at stake. Where you find value in your life, there, too, you're likely to be tender and vulnerable to pain. And so, avoiding feeling the grief that comes with loss means avoiding being fully in the relationship. Avoiding frustration means playing small, not trying too hard at too much. Avoiding anxiety or anger often means withdrawing from the world that could hurt us. Avoiding sadness means not stretching for something more. What if turning away from uncomfortable thoughts and feelings often means turning away from the things that matter to you?

So this is where we find ourselves:

- Bulimic behaviors may be helping you avoid some things in your life that are causing you pain, even if the bulimic behaviors work only for a little while and even if they cause more problems for you.

- You can't ignore your pain and go on with your life because, well, you don't have magic powers—normal humans get fixated easily on what hurts us.

- You can't just "stop thinking" about the things in your life that cause you pain as an alternative to these harmful behaviors.

- You're likely, if not certain, to encounter painful things in those areas of your life that you really care about, if for no other reason than simply because you care about them deeply.

- And, finally, your attempts to avoid the painful parts in these areas ultimately lead you to engage in these areas in a limited way or not at all.

In other words, as you try to avoid pain, the pain in your life grows and spreads. Your focus on it tightens. And before you realize it's happening, whole chunks of your life start to fall away.

Before we move on to the next thing, we invite you to take a moment and consider how this works for you. Consider again what you may have given up because of bulimia and what it would mean to you to get it back, at least in some way. Earlier we asked what you might do if your struggle with eating fell suddenly away. Take a moment now and reread that answer. You may catch a glimpse of some of the things that really matter to you, and find the areas in which you've paid the most serious costs because of your struggle.

HOW WE LEARN TO CHOOSE OUR PATHS

"Great," you might be thinking, "so the situation is that the way I've been eating doesn't work, and the ways I try to fix my eating don't work?" Well, yes. That's right. It's right, but not quite all. See, if you were able to notice something that you really care about, then you have already made your first move toward doing something different.

The context we carry with us in our thoughts and feelings is often painful. However, it's not *merely* painful. It's more than that. And the pain doesn't have to go away for us to notice what else is there. Take a deep breath and call to mind once more that last sunset that caught your eye. It's not hard to imagine that if you were to give yourself the time and the permission to pause to fully appreciate the next sunset of your life, a variety of experiences might show up. You might be awed by the colors. You might be exhilarated by the shadows. You might be reminded of the sunsets like this that you've missed. You might hurt over the people you wish you could share it with. And all of this, the painful and the precious, would make up the richness of the experience. This is not about focusing on what feels good and turning away from what hurts. It's about experiencing the world fully and turning toward the things we care about—on the days it feels good, and on the days it hurts.

Turns out we can learn to choose a new path that's not just about avoiding hurt. The more that we open ourselves up to our experiences, even those that hurt, the less important the hurt becomes. If you were terrified of water because you had almost drowned, but you wanted to work at a summer camp on a lake, one thing you might do would be to practice being near water. Initially, you'd feel fear—your heart would pound; you'd sweat and shake. You might be unable to work because you were so focused on avoiding the danger of the water. After some time, however, you'd notice the sunlight on the water and how it dances. You'd notice the cicadas buzzing, and you'd feel a breeze on your skin. Fear might still be there, but the experience would not be merely fear.

The same is true of the painful things you carry with you. You can learn to be with them without them taking over. And in that moment, you stop struggling and notice the world filling in around you. In that moment, the world is about more than your body or your eating. In that moment, you have choices. And when you notice choices, you find yourself free. This book is about finding that freedom.

CHAPTER 2

A Different Way of Doing Things

As we've said, ACT is not about solving problems or getting rid of pain. In fact, it's not about *getting rid* of anything. It's not even about getting rid of bulimia. "Wait a second," you might be thinking, "isn't that sort of the point?" Well, yes and no.

It's like this—there's no mystery as to what you would need to do to "get rid of bulimia." Stop binge eating. Stop compensatory behavior. And hey, job done. Even before you picked up this book, you knew what would have to change. But somehow, knowing that is just not enough. We want more for you.

See, there's that other piece of what doctors call "bulimia": body image difficulty. And your body image is part of the context that you carry with you, part of that pesky aspect of context that doesn't respond well when you try to change or avoid it. Remember our goofy "try not to think about a horse" request? What if we said instead, "Try not to think about those parts of your body you just hate"? That doesn't seem quite so goofy, does it? In fact, it probably feels pretty familiar. From an ACT perspective, trying to stop feeling bad—about your life or about your body—is what fuels bulimic behaviors. And we did, after all, promise you something different.

So, as strange as it sounds, "ACT for bulimia" is not about getting rid of bulimia. We bring this up because we don't even want getting rid of bulimia sneaking into your work here. The work we are going to do is about much, much more than that. What do we mean, more? Well, that depends on you.

REVISITING ACT'S PURPOSE AND GOAL: THE FLEXIBILITY TO LIVE A VALUED LIFE

Remember way back in the introduction, when we talked about the purpose of ACT as *valued living?* At the time, we talked about it simply as living a richer, more meaningful life. Now that you know a little more about where we are coming from, we can get a little more specific about where we are, where we're going, and what we hope to accomplish along the way.

Our Purpose: Commitment to Valued Living

From an ACT perspective, *valued living* is a pattern of actions that put you in touch with your values. By your *values*, we simply mean the things that matter to you—the things you choose to care about. Usually we talk about this in terms of various areas of life, like family, career, and spirituality.

VALUES: WHAT THEY ARE AND WHAT THEY AREN'T

A couple of points are important here. First, we're *not* talking about things you feel you *should* care about. Everybody grows up learning the world's ideas about what is important in life. Sometimes people really suffer because their life doesn't match the world's ideas about what life should look like. Values are not about figuring out what other people care about. They aren't even about *figuring out* what you care about. Remember, problem solving doesn't serve you very well in these instances. There's no "wrong" value. Values are what you choose to care about, without explanation or apology.

Also, when we say "care about," we are not talking about having thoughts and feelings. Remember, thoughts and feelings are the parts of context that we carry with us, but can't do a whole lot about. When we say "care about," we mean by taking action. A person could care about global warming and not do anything about it besides feel frustration or hopelessness and think, "Oh man, that really bites." We could also actively care about global warming in a number of actions we do throughout the day, from the way we travel, to the food we eat, to the things we buy.

In the same way, when we say "choose," we don't mean a one-time declaration that you just have to stick to after you say it. We mean actively choosing, in this moment, to care about something. And in this moment. And in this moment.

What if you could live the moments of your life rich with intention and meaning? Take a slow, deep breath here, and let what we're asking wash over you. These aren't the kind of questions that demand an answer. They are the kind of questions you breathe in and out. The kind of questions you sit in long enough to feel all the things that show up. What if the things that we asked of you in this book could help to move you toward that purpose? What if the work you do with this book could be part of *your* valued living? What might you do with that opportunity? Where might you go? What kind of person might you grow into? What if you could give yourself that gift just by leaning into the experiences we offer here? And breathe. What if.

COMMITMENT: THE GENTLE TURN BACK

Now we get into committing to valued living. We start with defining what we mean by commitment. When people use the word "commitment" out in the world, they use it to mean a promise to do something, sometimes a number of things. But there's more that comes with that. Commitment is often considered something to be feared and to be broken. There is a sense of burden that comes with commitment, and an expectation. People talk about commitment as though it shouldn't be made unless the person is certain it will be fulfilled. It's as though if your commitment is "honest," making that promise will somehow control your behavior, keeping you from straying from the behavior you promised. No wonder people are "scared of commitment"!

So throw out all that you know about commitment out in the world. When *we* say commitment, we're talking not about the words you say before, and the sense of burden that comes with it. We're talking about the act of returning to a pattern of valued living when you find yourself moving away. We believe that the single act of returning to that important thing you left behind typifies true commitment. The question is not "Will you turn away from things that matter to you?" The question is "Will you turn back?"

Our Goal: Psychological Flexibility

The work that we offer in this book will be about moving you toward living *your* values, and turning back when you find you're not. Inside the ACT perspective are some ideas about how best to do that. This is where the goal of ACT comes in: psychological flexibility. So often we move about our worlds without being aware of the things we are thinking, feeling, and doing, without being aware of ourselves or our freedom to choose. So often we narrow our focus to the things that hurt us and how to get away from them. And on the days when we look around and suddenly notice how far we are from the person we want to be, we very often turn away from that experience.

It's as if you suddenly found yourself lost in a forest. You'd need to spend a minute looking around, getting a sense of where you were. You'd need to take some time to choose a course. And if there were brambles or streams or fallen branches in the way, you'd have to be willing to move across them to get where you're trying to go.

From an ACT perspective, psychological flexibility involves being fully aware of and open to your ongoing experiences as a fully conscious human being as you act in a way that serves your values. The idea is that only when we are aware of what is present, and willing to experience it, are we able to move. Otherwise, we miss opportunities to act.

The broad goal of psychological flexibility is often broken up into six smaller goals. In addition to *valued living* and *committed action* are *being present, noticing self-as-context, looking past your thoughts*, and *accepting experience*. Let's take a moment to look at the four we haven't talked about. As you read over these brief descriptions, just notice what they bring up for you. Don't let yourself get stuck on any one of these if they don't quite make sense to you at first. We'll have plenty of time to explore them from the inside out.

- *Being present* involves noticing your ongoing experiences as they occur in and around you.

- *Seeing self-as-context* involves contacting the "you" that is more than the things you know *about* you.

- *Looking past your thoughts* involves noticing your thoughts without letting certain thoughts dominate your experience.

- *Accepting experience* involves being open to those thoughts and the feelings that come with them.

Together, these behaviors make up a way of being that can change as the situation calls for changing or stay the same when the situation calls for persistence. In short, you find yourself becoming more and more flexible. This flexibility means that even as the context changes, with different things happening and different thoughts and feelings coming up, you are free to continue working toward your values. What if you could find the flexibility to begin building a valued life? What if every moment included that chance? What if.

WITHOUT A PADDLE: WHAT OUR WORK MIGHT LOOK LIKE

So, how is all of this going to happen? How exactly will you use this book to help you choose and create a new path for yourself? How can just reading a book change your overall way of being? It can't. Remember, we are offering you an invitation, but we aren't going to be providing transportation. This is your work to do, and it's up to you how much you engage it and what kind of difference it makes.

Our Methods: Practice Brings Freedom

Our part in this work is pretty simple compared to yours. In each chapter, we will offer our ideas on how getting stuck works and how you might be able to find your way to a little more freedom, a little more life. We'll ask you to do different things to try on these ideas, to see your life in a little bit of a different way. Then we'll invite you to move past the ideas into the actual behavior change. Each chapter will offer specific things you can do to put these ideas into practice in a way that serves your values. Then we'll invite you to choose a commitment that could make a difference for you.

Some of the practices we'll describe are things you'll do with the book in front of you, using the CD or online audio we provided to guide you. Others invite you to close the book for a while and begin doing things differently out in your life. The effect this work has on you will depend entirely upon you.

Now, you should know that this work is going to be hard. Let's just get that out of the way now. We're going to make it simple and understandable, but some of the simplest, most common experiences are not easy. If we had to guess, very little of what we will ask of you will be easy. And it's not just because we are after your pain. Remember, right inside of the things you care about are the hurts you struggle with, and right inside of the hurts you struggle with are hints of the things you care about. It's not possible to do work that matters without rubbing up against things that are painful.

We could do work that was easy. We could tell you *about* behavior change and *about* how to do it. We could give you a couple of quick fix-it tips on seeking relief when life hurts. We could write you a nice, safe diet and exercise plan to follow. We could stay away from things that seem particularly personal or painful. We could keep things light. We could, but we won't.

Quite honestly, if we can't ask about things that are hard and confusing for you, if we can't invite you to try things that hurt, if we can't encourage you to take bold steps toward your values, our usefulness is pretty limited. Hurt is always present, and more so in things that matter to you. Learning to find freedom to choose valued living even in the most difficult of moments is inherent in our purpose and our goal. Teaching you this work while protecting you from hurt would be like having you watch someone ride a bike and take a spin down the driveway with training wheels, then sending you off to do the Tour de France with a firm clap on the back. It skips some steps between where you are and where you're headed, and we want this time you're putting in, this effort, to actually matter.

So in the moments when every part of your being says "no" to the thing we are asking you to sit with, we encourage you to pause gently for a moment and breathe, and call to mind your purpose for this work, how this work might serve your values. And breathe. And if you're not ready to move forward in a way that serves your values in that moment, give yourself a break, and come back when you're ready. It's not about forcing yourself off the high dive into the deep end. The nature of this work is such that if you don't freely choose it, you won't get the right results.

We'll put a hand on values here and there in every chapter. To start out, however, we'd like you to take a moment and let yourself come to rest on some small piece of your values. In other words, we'd like you to practice contacting your values right here, right now. One way of getting at this is by calling to mind a time when, maybe without even meaning to be, you were in touch with a value.

PRACTICE: SWEET SPOT (GUIDED MEDITATION)

■ Gently let your eyes close and take a couple of slow, deep breaths. Call to mind a moment in your life when that struggle you keep finding yourself in just fell away. A moment when you felt fully alive and aware in your own skin. A moment of sweetness in your life.

■ And breathe. It can be a moment long ago and far away, or it can be a bit of sweetness that came to you recently. It can be an important moment in your life or something simple that you often take for granted. If you find yourself struggling to pick the best moment or the one that makes the most sense, stop and breathe. Let yourself settle into a single, specific sweet spot.

■ When you've settled on a specific sweet spot, take note of all the little details of that moment, as if time slowed way down so you could take it all in. Imagine you could look through your eyes, stand in your shoes, in that moment. Notice the air around you—the temperature of it, whether it is breezy or still. Take a deep breath and draw in any smells that were present. Notice the light where you are, and the colors. Let yourself notice anyone who is with you—the look on their faces, the way they move. And breathe. With each breath, let yourself take in a new detail of that moment. If you can't remember, make up something specific that fits.

■ When you have called up enough details of the world around you in that sweet spot, turn your attention inward. Notice any feelings that are there in that moment of sweetness, as the world fills in around you. Let the feelings rise up inside you right now as if you were carrying them with you all this time and simply had to call upon them. Notice any sadness that comes with that sweetness. See if you can't make space for that to be here, too.

■ Take three slow, deep breaths as if you could breathe that moment in and carry it with you forever. And whenever you're ready, open your eyes, letting that sense of sweetness stay with you.

Now, if you're willing, consider what there was that was precious for you inside of that sweet spot. Be careful not to think too hard about this. If you find yourself hemming, hawing, and hesitating, take a deep breath and give yourself permission to do this "wrong." What was precious for you in that sweet moment? What made that moment sweet? What value or values did this point to?

Our Commitments: Setting the Compass

We've said that the work we will offer in this book is going to be hard, but that it will be *for* something. This purpose isn't something we can pick for you. We have our own ideas about what is important to us. If we knew you, we'd have hopes for where you might go and what you might find there. But even then, that wouldn't be what our work would be for. What will guide our work together, and make it so that we continue to move forward in the hardest moments, is your chosen values.

We invite you to take a moment now and consider what you choose for this work to be about.

PRACTICE: PICKING PURPOSE

- Start by calling to mind the answers you gave when we asked what you would do if you woke one morning to find that your struggle with eating and body image were to suddenly fall away. What did you see yourself doing? Take a moment and see yourself moving through your life with a sense of freedom. Where do you take yourself? What do you find there?

- Now call to mind once more the sweet spot you settled into just a few pages back. We invite you to ask yourself, what was precious to you inside of that moment? What was the source of all that sweetness? What brought that sense of life and of freedom? If you find yourself puzzling over this, reaching to find the "right" answer, or telling yourself this could never happen, take a few slow, deep breaths and give yourself permission to let this experience wash over you, without having to figure anything out.

- And whenever you're ready, we invite you to consider different areas of your life using the Valued Living Questionnaire (VLQ) below. If you are working in a notebook, you can copy the table below, or download a separate worksheet from http://20145.nhpubs.com.

VALUED LIVING QUESTIONNAIRE

Below are twelve areas of life that are valued by some people. We are concerned with your quality of life in each of these areas. You'll rate several aspects in regard to each area. Ask yourself the following questions when you make ratings in each area. Not everyone will value all of these areas, or value all areas the same. Rate each area according to your own personal view of it.

Possibility: How possible is it that something very meaningful could happen in this area of your life? Rate how possible you think it is on a scale of 1 to 10. 1 means that it isn't at all possible and 10 means that it is very possible.

Current importance: How important is this area at this time in your life? Rate the importance on a scale of 1 to 10. 1 means the area isn't at all important and 10 means that the area is very important.

Overall importance: How important is this area in your life as a whole? Rate the importance on a scale of 1 to 10. 1 means that the area isn't at all important and 10 means that the area is very important.

Action: How much have you acted in the service of this area during the past week? Rate your level of action on a scale of 1 to 10. 1 means you haven't been active at all with this value and 10 means you've been very active with this value.

Satisfied with level of action: How satisfied are you with your level of action in this area during the past week? Rate your satisfaction with your level of action on a scale of 1 to 10. 1 means you aren't at all satisfied and 10 means you're completely satisfied with your level of action in this area.

Concern: How concerned are you that this area won't progress as you want? Rate your level of concern on a scale of 1 to 10. 1 means that you aren't at all concerned and 10 means that you're very concerned.

	Possibility	Current Impor-tance	Overall Impor-tance	Action	Satisfied with Action	Concern
1. Family (other than marriage or parenting)						
2. Marriage, Couples, or Intimate relations						
3. Parenting						
4. Friends and Social Life						
5. Work						
6. Education and Training						
7. Recreation and Fun						
8. Spirituality						
9. Community Life						
10. Physical Self-Care (diet, exercise, and sleep)						
11. The Environment (caring for the planet)						
12. Aesthetics (art, literature, music, beauty)						

■ Now, take a breath and slowly, gently look back at your answers, not just in terms of the number ratings, but in terms of the experiences that guided your ratings. You may find yourself second-guessing your ratings or wanting to change this one or that. We invite you to sit with that doubt or that urge, just noticing what comes up as you review your answers.

■ Which areas of life are most important to you right now? Which ones are you most concerned about? Which areas of life feel impossible? Where are you spending most of your efforts these days? In what areas of your life is there a mismatch between its importance and your satisfaction with your own action?

■ If working through this book were to help you to make meaningful and extraordinary changes in your life, in what area of your life would those changes occur?

■ Now, if you are willing, take a moment to write down a value that you would be willing to work toward, using one of the categories in the VLQ or your own words. If you'd like to be bold, pick an area where you have room to grow, like one that is important to you, but where your thoughts say growth is impossible.

■ I value: _____

Now consider what commitment to the work we are offering might look like for you. Is it reading a chapter a week? Practicing for ten minutes a day? Is it ten pages every Sunday and practicing three times a week? Is it a chapter over two weeks but at least a page a day? Is it something, either reading or practicing or both, every third Tuesday? Is it finishing the book in three months and journaling every day on how it's affecting your life? Think about what you will commit to. See if you can't stretch a little. Go for something that seems almost out of reach, like a vase on a high shelf. There's no "right" commitment to make, and you can always change your commitment. And remember, the nature of commitment is the pattern of turning back, so give yourself permission to pick something you might mess up.

I commit to this work in service of my value of _____

_____

by _____

If you made it through the practices above and are still reading, we offer you our congratulations. Seriously. This is hard stuff. There's something really terrifying about putting your values out there, even if you know no one is going to read what you've written. These moments in which you choose to serve your values are important. They are what make up valued living. And if you didn't write anything down, we want to remind you that these are all open invitations. Walk-ins are welcome, and you are always invited to stay.

Six Opportunities for Change

CHAPTER 3

Right Here, Right Now: Learning to Be

Most of us can easily call to mind a time when we suddenly "woke up" to something going on around us. Maybe you suddenly became aware of someone calling to you, trying to get your attention. Maybe you suddenly realized you had no idea what was going on in the movie you'd been watching. Maybe you suddenly noticed you'd passed up an exit on a route you've taken a thousand times. Maybe you've gone a couple of pages in this book and suddenly recognized that you had no idea what you'd read.

Typically we call this distance from the present "mind wandering" or "zoning out." There are tons of examples, and this looks a little different for everyone. Some people "daydream" and experience vivid images of dreamlike fantasies when they're bored. We call people "distractible" or "inattentive" if mind wandering prevents them from focusing. Some people worry or ruminate, getting lost in trying to solve problems of the past or the future. Some people "shut down" or "check out" when something upsetting happens. People talk about "being on autopilot" when they carry out actions without being fully aware of them. Some people talk about "being absorbed" in playing a video game or writing a paper to the extent that they don't know what's going on around them. If you get absorbed in contacting certain perceptions, like chewing your lip, tapping your pencil, gazing at lights, or repeating a word or sound to yourself, some call it "stimming" or "self-stimulatory behavior." People argue about how these are the same or different or related behaviors, but the thing that is common to all of these is that you are unaware of the events going on around you. And if you're like most people, this is just something that happens. Actually, if you're like most people, this is something that happens a lot.

Research suggests that we spend about 20 to 30 percent of our time with our minds wandering, depending on our age (Giambra 2000) and what kind of task we're engaged in (for example, Kane et al. 2007). And we get away with it. It seems that most of what we do in our daily lives, we can do without paying much attention at all. Apart from missing our turn every once in a while, this seems to work out okay.

It works out okay except for one problem. Earlier, we described behavior as being learned, and learning as depending on context, or the events happening around the behavior. It turns out that if you are not in contact with the context, it's pretty difficult to learn anything. And we don't just mean zoning out in class and missing the review on fractions. We mean learning how to be effective in the world. To use our earlier examples, it would be pretty hard to learn to pat the baby on the back if you were so freaked out by the crying that you didn't notice what calmed the baby and what didn't. You wouldn't learn to try channel 42 if you were flipping through the channels without noticing what was on. The same is true of our effectiveness at valued living. When we aren't present, we miss stuff. And sometimes the things that we miss are opportunities to pursue something we really care about.

HOW BEING PRESENT RELATES TO EATING

Eating begins as a relatively automatic behavior. For example, most humans are born with the reflexes to turn toward things that touch their cheeks and to suck on things that enter their mouths. Quickly, however, those reflexes are shaped based on their consequences. Certain kinds of sucking work better for getting milk than other kinds of sucking, so that behavior becomes more likely. As our diet varies, our eating changes based on tastes and textures, changing demands, and other aspects of context. We learn to clamp up when we see green beans to avoid the taste. We learn to hold our tongues down to eat from spoons. We learn to "clean our plate" to gain praise.

Eventually, we learn to carry context with us, and our eating is affected by our *ideas* of its consequences. We might avoid ice cream even though we love the taste because of the idea that it is fattening. We might eat organic berries even though they are more expensive because of the idea that they haven't been exposed to pesticides. It seems that much of what we learn about food and eating is not from consequences we've directly experienced, but from these ideas of consequences, even when we can't describe them. For example, a person might eat biscuits because they remind her of her grandmother, but be able to say only that for some reason she prefers them to toast.

Gradually, the kinds of contexts that control our eating behavior become more and more varied, and paying attention in a certain way to some aspects of context becomes increasingly important. If most of the consequences that control your eating have to do with praise (for example, "good job cleaning your plate"), then paying attention to people around you while eating has become more important than paying attention to feelings of fullness. If most of the consequences that control your eating have to do with avoiding feelings of fullness, then paying attention to feelings in your body while eating has become more important than paying attention to the tastes of the foods you're eating. If most of the consequences that control your eating have to do with avoiding feeling bad, then paying attention to your thoughts and feelings while eating has become more important than paying attention to just about anything else.

NOTICING BEING PRESENT AND NOT BEING PRESENT

Overall, individuals who struggle with bulimic behaviors tend to be more likely to show difficulties with being present than those who don't. Often, people report feeling disconnected from their thoughts, feelings, and bodily sensations when they overeat. When this happens over and over, people can tend to drift away from the present whenever they eat. For some, this becomes more and more common in other situations besides eating, especially those that are difficult.

Practicing Noticing

But it doesn't matter so much here what is common to those struggling with bulimic behaviors. What matters is *your* experience. We'd like to take some time now and invite you to practice noticing being present and not being present. This practice is in four parts. You'll need something to read for the first part, and a snack (a small serving of your choice) for the third part. You'll also need an interval timer (such as that available online at http://speedbagforum.com/timer or for iPhone at http://intervals app.com/).

PRACTICE: NOTICING BEING PRESENT (GUIDED PRACTICE)

PART I

- If you are using a timer, set the timer for three minutes and set the interval alarm to go off every fifteen seconds. Start the timer and begin reading. When the interval alarm sounds, mark a "+" if you were attending to what you were reading and a "−" if you were not. When you notice you are not attending, return your focus to your reading.

Interval 1: _____

Interval 2: _____

Interval 3: _____

Interval 4: _____

Interval 5: _____

Interval 6: _____

Interval 7: _____

Interval 8: _____

Interval 9: _____

Interval 10: _____

Interval 11: _____

Interval 12: _____

▪ Count the "−" marks and write that number here: _____

PART 2

▪ If you are using a timer, leave it set as is. This time when you start the timer, simply focus on your breath—the physical sensations of breathing. When the interval alarm sounds, mark a "+" if you were attending to your breathing and a "−" if you were not. When you notice you are not attending, return your focus to your breath.

Interval 1: _____

Interval 2: _____

Interval 3: _____

Interval 4: _____

Interval 5: _____

Interval 6: _____

Interval 7: _____

Interval 8: _____

Interval 9: _____

Interval 10: _____

Interval 11: _____

Interval 12: _____

▪ Count the "–" marks and write that number here: _____

PART 3

▪ If you are using a timer, leave it set as is. This time when you start the timer, begin eating the food slowly, noticing every detail about eating—the taste, texture, and temperature of the food, what it feels like in your jaw to chew, and so on. When the interval alarm sounds, mark a "+" if you were attending to your eating and a "–" if you were not. When you notice you are not attending, return your focus to your food.

Interval 1: _____

Interval 2: _____

Interval 3: _____

Interval 4: _____

Interval 5: _____

Interval 6: _____

Interval 7: _____

Interval 8: _____

Interval 9: _____

Interval 10: _____

Interval 11: _____

Interval 12: _____

▪ Count the "–" marks and write that number here: _____

PART 4

▓ If you are using a timer, keep it set at three minutes, but this time, don't set an interval alarm. When you start the timer, close your eyes and focus on your breath again. When you notice you are not attending to your breath, make a small mark below, and return your focus to your breath.

▓ Count the marks you made and write that number here: _____ . Were you more present to your breath or less than in Part 2?

Now take a minute to consider your experiences in all of the parts of this practice.

▓ How was this practice for you?

▓ What did you notice about this practice? Was it harder for you to stay present in some parts than in others?

▓ When you were not present, what was going on for you? If you don't remember, we encourage you to try the exercise again, this time making a point to notice not only if you were present but what you were doing when you were not present. If you can remember, write down some of the distractions or mental activites that showed up and pulled you from the present:

_____

_____

_____

_____

_____

_____

Noticing as Valued Living

We encourage you to repeat this kind of practice out in your life at least a few times with different kinds of activities, in different kinds of situations. Set your watch or phone to beep every ten minutes, and just notice whether or not you are present to the activity you are doing. Are you paying attention to the movie you are watching? Are you noticing the sights around you on the highway? Are you listening to the person who is talking to you? Just practice noticing where your mind is in any one moment. How about in the situations that are connected to things really important to you? Are you fully present, ready to receive anything extraordinary that comes along?

VALUED PRACTICE

If you think it might be useful to you, we invite you to make a specific commitment to apply this practice to your values. Pause, take a few deep breaths, and think of at least one situation in your life in which opportunities for valued living might come up. These would be situations in which there is something important to you at stake, but it might be easy to miss or mess up if you weren't really present. For example, you might value being a mother and wish you could be more engaged when you're doing homework with your child. You might value your family relationships and wish you could enjoy family meals like you used to. Now imagine yourself in that situation, and watch yourself as you move through your world. How present do you appear? Looking from the outside, how can you tell? Who else notices?

Allow yourself to breathe the scene in and out three times, then write your commitment below. For example, if you were the absent mother above, you might commit to scheduling a particular hour for homework three days this week and setting your watch on a ten-minute interval, noticing whether or not you were present when the alarm sounded. Try to pick something that's doable, but still a challenge, and related to the value you chose. Don't rush this process of choosing your commitment. And remember, when you turn away from your commitment, the next thing to do is simply turn back.

In service of my value of _____ , I commit to practicing noticing being present by _____

_____

_____

_____

Use the chart below to record your progress. There is space for five practice sessions. We suggest you do at least three. We also ask you to give yourself permission to hang out here with this commitment for a while, not moving forward in this work until you feel that you've begun to satisfy your commitment to yourself and are ready to move on.

	(Check below when complete)	Comments
Session 1		
Session 2		
Session 3		
Session 4		
Session 5		

FINDING THE NOW: RETURNING TO THE PRESENT

Now that you've begun to notice *in the moment* the difference between being present and not being present, we'd like to move on to that shift back to being present. We want to be clear here that the noticing we practiced in the last part actually involves being present. In other words, you have to get present to notice you aren't present.

Your contact with the present moment is made up of all of your ongoing experiences rushing by at any one moment. The present moment is not something you can hold on to, or a place where you can set down roots. Imagine a train rushing by: if you were to grab on to one of the cars as it passed, it wouldn't stay put. You (and it) would be whisked off. It's the same here; if you try to hold on to a particular piece of your experience as it shows up, before you can wrap your hands around it all the way, it's no longer in the present. Something compelling shows up, like the thought, "There I am, being disgusting again." And you can hardly help but try to grab on to that one. It hurts so bad and feels so true. You try to wrap your mind around it enough to disprove or explain it. And before you know it, you are whisked away like you'd grabbed on to a train car.

It's also not like you can return to the present once and for all and be done with it. Being whisked around by your experience is the typical state of affairs. It seems like it might be going somewhere important, but often we can't see a thing if we're dragging alongside it, holding on for dear life, flapping against the car over and over. And we spend most of our lives like this. "Am I disgusting? I am. Just look at my stomach. I should be doing more exercise. Yeah, I'm gonna go back to the gym. That'll be good. But how could I fit that in? Well, I could go in the morning. Let's see, if I lost a pound a week..." And there you go.

Being present is something you *do*, over and over, moment by moment. Technically, it's bringing *flexible* and *focused* attention to your experiences as they occur. Like sitting on a hill next to the train, you are able to shift your attention easily from one experience to the next, then the next, then the next. You might regard one train car a little longer than the next, or sometimes have to watch them rush by without being able to really tell one from the other. And this becomes easier and easier to do the more you practice.

Practicing Returning to the Present

Most people think about practicing being present only when they notice themselves having trouble staying present. Usually this comes up when there's something difficult going on and being present means contacting that. And although being present in moments that matter is sort of the point, that's more likely to happen when you've practiced under easier conditions.

There are many different forms that this kind of practice can take. Some folks prefer to stick with a simple breathing meditation in which the only instruction is to notice their breath. You should be getting pretty familiar with that act of pausing to notice your breath when things start to feel tight or rushed. Practicing can make finding those breaths when you need them a little easier. If you are using the CD, skip to the track called "Finding Your Breath." If not, you may want to read through the instructions before you begin, so you don't have to interrupt your practice to read the instructions. For this practice, you'll need your timer.

PRACTICE: FINDING YOUR BREATH (GUIDED MEDITATION)

- Set your timer for five minutes.

- Start by letting your eyes gently close, as you draw a slow, deep breath. And as you take that air into your body, let your body fall still for just a few moments here. And as you release that air from your body, see if you can't feel yourself settle in here. In your skin, in your chair, in this room, in this moment right now. And breathe.

- And as you breathe, simply notice what it feels like to draw a breath in, and to release. How it feels when the air hits your nostrils or lips, the pressure in your lungs in that moment between inhaling and exhaling, the shift in your muscles as you pull your abdomen in and push the air from your body. And breathe.

- Now see if you can notice each aspect of this experience of breathing:

- Notice the temperature of the air on your lips or nostrils on the way in, and on the way out. And breathe.

- Notice the tension in your chest as your lungs fill, and as they empty. And breathe.

- Notice your abdomen push out with the breath in, and pull in with each breath out. And breathe.

- Notice the sounds your breathing makes as the air rushes by your lips or nostrils. Notice the difference in the sound when you draw the air in, and when you release it. Notice the silent moments between inhaling and exhaling. And breathe.

- Notice any smells you take in as you breathe, and any taste the air leaves in the back of your throat. And breathe.

- Allow your attention to come to rest upon each of these aspects of noticing your breath. And when you notice your mind beginning to wander, gently return to your breath until the timer signals the end of the practice.

Most people find this practice harder than it sounds. Five minutes can feel like an eternity when your only job is to notice your breath. Then again, most people don't have trouble noticing things they've never noticed before about the breathing they do every day. If you found yourself really struggling with this practice, it may be worth coming back to it. Setting aside time for just one five-minute practice a day can make it easier to call on your breath when you really need it.

You may prefer more variability or more guidance. From an ACT perspective, being present involves flexible focus, so practicing being present involves practicing focusing here, then gently transitioning to focusing there, then gently transitioning to focusing over there. And when attention is pulled to a scary thought or to a sudden sound in the room, it's gently gathered up and brought back to focus.

One way of practicing this is to focus on a particular sense, like hearing, touch, taste, or smell. In this practice, we will focus on our experience of touch. Rather than returning to our breath, we will return to the sensation of touch present in any one moment. Again, it may be useful to read through the exercise before you begin.

PRACTICE: TOUCHING THE NOW
(GUIDED MEDITATION)

- Set your timer for five minutes.

- Let your eyes gently close and draw three deep, full breaths. As you breathe, notice what it feels like to take air into your body.

- Start by focusing on the feeling of the air rushing by the skin on your nose or lips. Notice the temperature change as you draw air in, hold it, and release it. Take three breaths, bringing your attention back when it wanders away. And breathe.

- Now gently shift your attention to your chest and midsection. Notice the way they move as they draw the air in and out. Feel the muscles pull as you draw air in and loosen as you release. And breathe.

- Notice the skin on your chest and midsection as they move with your breathing. Notice the changing pressure of your clothes on your body. And breathe.

- Now see if you can open your awareness just a bit to allow yourself to notice the whole feeling of breathing. Notice the air rushing past the skin on your nose or lips, the movement of the muscles in your chest and midsection, the changing pressure of your clothes on your skin, and other physical sensations that change slowly, back and forth, with your breath. And breathe.

- If you find your attention being pulled to another feeling or another part of your body, gently return to the physical experience of breathing in and out.

- Whenever you feel that you are settled into a sense of what it feels like to breathe, gently shift your attention to your hands. Notice the temperature of your hands in different areas—tiny shifts in temperature between your fingers and palms. And as you breathe, see if you can notice the areas of your hands that are warmer than the rest.

- Now notice the different amounts of pressure on different areas of your hands, starting with the most pressure and working your way back to the areas of your hands that have nothing touching them or just the lightest contact. And breathe.

- Notice any areas of your hands that have pain or discomfort. Let your attention gently shift to any areas of tension in the muscles there in your fingers, any stiffness that is there. Scan your hands for any stinging or burning on the skin of your hands. And breathe.

- Next, see if you can open up your awareness to the entire physical experience of your hands. Without moving them, let the sensations of temperature, pressure, and pain rise to the front of your awareness.

- If you find your attention being pulled to another feeling or another part of your body, gently return to the physical experience of your hands.

- Repeat this exercise with your feet, your mouth, or other areas of your body until the timer sounds.

Now, there is nothing special about returning to your breath or bringing your attention back to physical sensations. In fact, we encourage you to start here, then practice in the same way with your other senses. In the beginning, having a particular subject to focus on smelling or tasting or hearing can help you to stay with the task. It might be most useful to practice with each of your senses at least a couple of times, giving yourself a chance to get to know what works for you.

Use the chart below to record your practices. Remember, your goal is to build present-moment focus as a skill that you carry with you. You'll get the most benefit out of this work by practicing it regularly so that anytime, anywhere, in any situation, you can notice that you are not present and return to the events going on around you and within you in that moment.

	(Check below when complete)	Comments
Touch: Session 1		
Touch: Session 2		
Hearing: Session 1		
Hearing: Session 2		
Sight: Session 1		
Sight: Session 2		
Taste: Session 1		
Taste: Session 2		
Smell: Session 1		
Smell: Session 2		

As you practice, you may find that it's easier for you to practice present-moment focus with some kinds of sensations than with others. For example, you may find yourself much less distracted by sounds in the room than by physical sensations. Sometimes, when you find yourself struggling to get present to a certain sensation, it's because that sensation is difficult for you in some way. Many people who struggle with body image and eating difficulties find it particularly difficult to be present with certain tastes, smells, and physical sensations and with their own physical appearance. We'll return to getting present to these kinds of experiences in the next chapter. For now, present-moment focus will be easiest for you to practice with things that are not particularly painful to you.

WHEN WE FIND PAIN IN THE NOW

You may also find, upon getting present, that you have thoughts or feelings come up that you didn't even realize were in there. You might end the exercise feeling sad or anxious. Every time you practice present-moment focus, you might be faced with your disappointment about how things are going for you, or your judgments of how you're handling your relationships. You might find yourself not wanting to practice present-moment focus because you don't particularly like the way you tend to feel afterward.

It's not easy to settle into what's present when what's present is difficult. However, we would suggest that this kind of exercise doesn't make feelings come up that aren't present already. It's like it's dark over there in that corner, and what these exercises do is give you a flashlight. What if these difficult thoughts and feelings are not only there whether or not you are aware of them, but they are pushing your behavior around, even when you don't know they are there? You might call to mind a day when you found yourself particularly sensitive to frustration, like any little thing that went wrong sent you spinning, or a day when you found yourself being nasty to someone you care about. Often when we stop and let ourselves become aware of what's present for us, we find some concern simmering there. We notice that we're more upset about that check bouncing than we'd thought. We're more worried about that sick uncle than we knew. We're more afraid about moving to a new place than we ever expected.

Returning to the Present as Valued Living

On some days, in some situations, not being aware of difficult thoughts and feelings might not matter all that much. You might not be as quick to finish something or as sensitive to people around you, but many of us get along pretty well even when we've got hard things going on. There are, however, a number of situations in which those thoughts and feelings push us away from the things that really matter to us. There are a number of situations in which those thoughts and feelings push us away from opportunities for valued living.

VALUED PRACTICE

Look back to the commitment you made to practice noticing when you are and are not present in a particular situation that is somehow connected to your values. Pause, take a few deep breaths, and call to mind the situation that you identified and the practice you did. Maybe you have a sense of how hard it is for you to be present in that situation, what it looks like when you aren't present, and the effect of that on your life. For example, you might have realized how often you "zone out" when your friends come to you with struggles.

You might have recognized how rarely you are really engaged in your work. You might have seen how focusing on solving a problem or completing a task has made you completely unavailable to the people around you. Make a few notes below that describe what "going away" looked like for you in the valued practice you did, and what cost that had:

_____

_____

_____

_____

Now, we invite you to extend the commitment you made before to not only noticing when you are not present, but returning to the present. Try to imagine particular things that you could return to when you drifted away. Like the flashing beacon in the lighthouse to the sailor, imagine that these particular things could call your attention back. You might choose things specific to the situation you chose. For example, if you chose interactions with your partner, you might return to his or her eyes when you find yourself drifting away. As an alternative, you might choose one of the sensations that seemed easy to return to for you, such as your breath or the sensations in your hands.

When I notice I am not present, I can choose to return to: _____

_____

Just as in the practices above, our purpose here is not to focus rigidly on one aspect of your experience so that everything else goes away. The sailor doesn't stare at the beacon in the lighthouse indefinitely. The purpose is to return your attention to that event in the present, then open your attention to anything else that shows up.

In service of my value of _____ , I commit to practicing returning to the present moment by:

_____

_____

_____

_____

_____

Use the chart below to record your progress. Once more, we've provided space for five practice sessions, and we suggest you do at least three. Again, we invite you to take your time in exploring this commitment. The next chapter will shift to another component of psychological flexibility and will build on the present-moment work you've done. There's plenty to experience here, and your valued life is worth it.

	(Check below when complete)	**Comments**
Session 1		
Session 2		
Session 3		
Session 4		
Session 5		

We started this chapter off by noting how often people drift away from the things that they are doing and experiencing in the present moment. For most people, this is so common that they don't even notice it anymore, let alone make any attempt to change it. So, congratulations! You've begun a piece of work that just about everyone could benefit from but that most people don't ever consider doing. And our bet is, if you stay with it long enough, you'll find extraordinary things in the present moment that you might have missed otherwise.

CHAPTER 4

Where It All Takes Place: Noticing Self-as-Context

From the ancient Greek maxim "Know thyself" to the quizzes in women's magazines, there's a common understanding that:

1. We don't automatically know ourselves.

2. Getting to know ourselves is a good thing.

So, how about it? Who are you? It's a big question, isn't it? Take a minute and record below a few of the things you might say if you answered that question. There are no right or wrong answers here. We're not going to reveal to you that you are, in fact, a bad friend, too jealous, or a prude. Just read the beginning of the sentence, "I am," aloud to yourself, and write down the first things that come to you in the blanks below.

1. I am _____ .

2. I am _____ .

3. I am _____ .

4. I am _____ .

5. I am _____ .

6. I am _____ .

Now take a look at your answers. What kinds of things did you write down? Everyone will answer this a little differently. Maybe you wrote down demographic information—your age, your race, your gender: "I am twenty-nine. I am white. I am a female." Maybe you wrote down things you do—your jobs and hobbies: "I am a waitress. I am a runner." Maybe you wrote down your different roles in relationships: "I am a daughter. I am a friend." Or your membership in a community: "I am a Louisianian. I am a Democrat. I am a Lutheran." Or your mood: "I am depressed. I am tired."

ONCE UPON A TIME: THE STORIES OF YOU

Regardless of what you wrote in those six blanks, you could probably complete six more "I am" statements with little trouble. One of the reasons that the question is a hard one is because each and every one of us is walking around with a number of pretty complex stories about who we are, who we definitely are not, and how we got that way. Each one of the statements you created is a story, a little piece of your self-concept, a glimpse into how you see yourself.

And these stories can feel pretty important. We clutch some of them close. We shove some of them as far out of reach as we can manage. Some stories we share with others, maybe eagerly, maybe hesitantly. Some stories we tuck away while working really hard to prove them false. Some people would say that our stories are, in fact, *us*.

Sometimes, however, we come to places in our lives where our stories are not enough. Sometimes life hands us something unexpected, and we don't have a story that tells us how we get up and keep going. Sometimes we look out at our lives before us and find ourselves dissatisfied with whom our stories tell us to be. Some days, we look back on our lives and see where the stories we have about ourselves have failed us, have fallen short of the life we are trying to live. Often we find ourselves fighting to change the story. But maybe there's more than a bunch of old stories. Maybe *you* are more.

Noticing Your Stories

Before we launch into too much explaining, we invite you to practice taking a look at your own stories of you. You'll start by building on the exercise from the beginning of this chapter. This time, however, you'll take a bit more time settling in before you begin writing, and you'll include not only "I am" but also "I am not."

PRACTICE: I AM/I AM NOT
(GUIDED MEDITATION AND PRACTICE)

- Set your timer for five minutes.

- Before you start the timer, close your eyes and take a few slow, deep breaths, taking a moment to notice how it feels to draw the air into your lungs and to release it.

- When you feel yourself present in the now, take five deep breaths. Breathe in slowly, letting the words "Who. Am. I." rise up one at a time and linger. Pause gently, briefly… notice any tension in your body. Then breathe out slowly, letting the words "I. Am." rise up and hang like a statement unfinished.

- As you take these five gentle breaths, notice your mind scrambling to fill in the blanks this way or that— pulling the words together into questions and answers. And if you find yourself trying to silence certain thoughts or pushing them here or there, see if you can't gently let that struggle go, letting yourself simply notice what shows up as you breathe.

- At the end of five breaths, let your eyes open, start the timer, and complete the following statements, one at a time, for five minutes. Don't think too hard about what you write in any one blank. The point is not to write things because they are positive or negative, true or false. It is simply to write what shows up. If you find yourself filtering certain things out, or puzzling over what this or that might mean, pause your timer and take one or two deep breaths. Notice how difficult it can be to just observe the different ways of seeing yourself that come up.

1. I am _____.

2. I am not _____.

3. I am _____.

4. I am not _____.

5. I am _____.

6. I am _____.

7. I am _____.

8. I am not _____.

9. I am not _____.

10. I am _____.

11. I am not _____.

12. I am not _____.

13. I am not _____.

14. I am not _____.

15. I am _____.

16. I am not _____.

17. I am _____.

18. I am _____.

19. I am _____.

20. I am not _____.

21. I am not _____.

22. I am not _____.

23. I am _____.

24. I am not _____.

25. I am _____.

26. I am not _____.

27. I am not _____.

28. I am _____.

29. I am _____.

30. I am _____.

31. I am not _____.

32. I am _____.

33. I am _____.

34. I am not _____.

35. I am not _____.

36. I am not _____.

37. I am not _____.

38. I am _____.

39. I am _____.

40. I am not _____.

41. I am _____.

42. I am not _____.

43. I am _____.

44. I am not _____.

45. I am _____.

46. I am _____.

47. I am not _____.

48. I am _____.

49. I am _____.

50. I am not _____.

▨ When you hear your timer, regardless of how much you've written down, take a deep breath and put your pencil down. If you complete all the statements before your timer goes off, simply stop and put your pencil down. And breathe. Let your eyes close, and take five slow, deep breaths before reading on. And whenever you're ready, open your eyes.

So... Now you know your stories, right? Well, close enough. Of course, this is just a tiny sample of all the self-stories you have floating around in your head. You could probably fill another fifty blanks. And another. And another. And still not be done. But perhaps you can start to recognize, in the words you wrote down, and (perhaps even more so) in the words you couldn't bring yourself to write down, the echo of your story.

How Stories Matter

Some of our stories just don't influence us very much. They feel true enough, but they don't really carry much weight. Many of our stories, however, do. Maybe you have a story that you are "not a math person." How might you deal with having to take a math test for a new job or education opportunity?

Maybe you have a story that you are a "great friend." How might you react when someone accuses you of being selfish? Maybe you have a story that you are "unlovable." How might you react when someone you're interested in doesn't call when they said they would?

We all have stories we carry around with us that keep us from moving freely about our lives. These stories feel massive and heavy. We tend to live our lives around them, as if under their gravitational influence. Without our even realizing it, some stories begin to limit who we are, where we go, and what we get to do. For example, if your story involves your being introverted, you might miss an opportunity to get to know a new friend, help someone you care about, or contribute to a cause you believe in because it seems like you'd need to be outgoing to do a good job.

LIMITING LIFE: THE STORIES THAT PULL

Psychologists have long been interested in how our stories (usually called *self-concepts*) can influence our behavior. The main goal they've been after has been sorting out what kinds of stories tend to limit us and how we can change that.

The first step to shaking free of the hold those stories have on your life is to begin noticing your stories and which ones have that pull on your behavior. It doesn't seem to be an issue of negativity or positivity. For example, some stories about how competent we are, how easy things will be for us, and what great things lie ahead may help us to stay motivated in difficult situations. These same stories, however, might keep us from being able to see and learn from our own mistakes. Likewise, some stories about how incompetent we are, how hard things will be for us, and what horrible things lie ahead may help us to work harder than the next guy. These same stories, however, might keep us from pursuing extraordinary things that seem out of reach.

It also doesn't seem to be an issue of accuracy or inaccuracy. Some of the most dangerous stories are the ones that most would say are as true as they get. It might be really, really true that we are smart, sensitive, creative, and hardworking. But if we can't see the times when we aren't (and there will be times when we aren't), we're likely to alienate the people around us and not likely to learn how not to. By the same token, we might have all the evidence in the world that we are stupid, or insensitive, or close-minded, or lazy. But if we can't see opportunities to be more than that, even if we don't believe them, we're bound to be stupid, insensitive, close-minded, and lazy forever.

How Stories Relate to Eating

For many people who struggle with their eating, how they eat and how they look are important themes in their stories. It's not hard to look back and see a time in your life when eating in certain ways meant you were "good." Maybe cleaning your plate was a surefire way to win your dad's praise and affection. Maybe Mom fussed over your picky eating. Maybe your big sister called you "a pig." At some point, *how you eat* became more important to *who you are* than you would want. Emphasizing appearance can work the same way. Maybe you were always told how "cute" or "thin" you were. Or maybe you noticed that you weren't the one being told that. Maybe you were taught to take great care in your appearance. Maybe you were the "fat kid" among your friends. Maybe your aunt commented that you were "too thin" every time she saw you. At some point, *how you look* became more important to *who you are* than you would want.

And over time, you learned to manage these stories by managing your eating. You might feel best about yourself when you're restricting your eating, or when you notice you're losing weight. You might feel worst about yourself when you're binge eating or when you notice you're gaining weight. And if you've struggled with all this for a while, you probably feel somewhat ambivalent about anything to do with eating and appearance.

As with all the stories we have about ourselves, the important thing is not what the stories say, or even how they make you feel. It is how they influence your actions. And only you can really know which stories affect your life and why. The ones that really pull on you might not affect somebody else that much. And you might be fine with stories that would really disrupt someone else's life. It may be beneficial to not only to think about your stories in a conceptual, intellectual way, but to practice noticing them in the moment they come up.

Noticing Pulls

In this practice, by reading over the statements you generated above with a present-moment focus, you will notice how some of your stories compel you.

PRACTICE: PULL-MARKING
(GUIDED PRACTICE)

Before you begin, locate your list of "I am's" and "I am not's" from the last practice, and find a timer and something to write with.

- Start this practice by gently letting your eyes close and taking five slow, deep breaths. As you breathe, notice all the things going on in your body. As you draw air in and out, see if you can watch the flurry of activity taking place in your body even as you sit here, still and quiet. And breathe.

- Now, look back to the statements you created. Set your timer for one minute. During this minute, scan what you wrote casually, without looking for anything in particular. Notice which statements grab your attention as you peruse the list. When you feel yourself pulled by an urge to analyze, or to explain, or to relish, or to erase a certain statement, take a breath and make a small mark next to that statement.

■ When your minute is over, close your eyes and take one deep, slow breath, again taking time to notice the sensations in your body in that moment.

■ Open your eyes and return your attention to the statements you just created. This time, you don't need to set the timer. Just read each one quietly to yourself, noticing how it feels to read it out loud. Again, notice which statements grab your attention in some way. When you come to a statement you feel the urge to skip over, or to change, or to explain, take a breath and make a small mark next to that statement. The same goes for when you come to statements you want to read, to relish, or to describe to someone. Take a breath and make a small mark by those numbers. Finally, notice any statements that seem to conflict with other statements, and make a small mark next to those.

■ Finally, let your eyes close one last time, and take a few more gentle breaths.

Whenever you're ready, look back over the marks you made, noting any patterns that emerge. It may be useful to ask yourself a few specific questions:

■ What kind of statements did you mark? Is there something similar about all of them?

■ Are the statements you marked all part of the same story? Or is each one connected to a bigger story, like icebergs under the surface?

■ What's missing from these statements you marked? Are there stories you didn't write down that are coming up now?

■ Which of your pulls are the strongest?

■ Which of your pulls come up most often, in the most situations?

Take a moment and write down the stories you carry that seem most relevant to your life right now. Whether they come up often, pull strongly when they do come up, or just seem to be important to the life you're trying to live, it may be useful to jot them down here.

I have these stories that I carry with me:

_____

_____

_____

_____

_____

_____

_____

If you were able to jot a few things down, great. If you find yourself struggling with this ("Is this really a pull? Well, this is so much like this, I shouldn't put it down. Maybe this whole thing is not really a strong pull. I mean, it's strong, but not really strongest…"), let yourself step away from the task from an hour, or a few hours, or even a day. Come back to your list fresh and do the practice again.

Noticing Stories and Pulls as Valued Living

Considering how *your* stories about yourself influence *your* behavior is a big job. It can easily feel overwhelming to look at your life in this way. But this is not a one-time task. "Okay. I thought about how my stories influence my life. Job done! Next chapter!" The purpose of noticing your stories and pulls is not to gather information. Knowing what they are and that they are there doesn't in and of itself change how they work in your life. The act of noticing, however, does.

So noticing the pulls your stories have on your behavior is less a matter of discovering something and more a matter of opening yourself up to seeing what shows up over time. It's sort of like the difference between throwing curtains open to see what's out there versus ripping down the curtains and opening up the window. You're not going to hurry up and memorize everything you see out there so you can pull the curtains closed again. You're also not going to be standing there in front of this window all day, every day, soaking up every little change. But sometimes, when you pass it on your way to somewhere important, you might notice a shift there. Sometimes, before you step out into the world, it may be useful to consider what you're likely to encounter. One way to begin jimmying that window open is to continue the practice of noticing pulls in the moment.

You noticed your pulls in the last section by paying attention to urges to act on certain statements you'd written. But feeling an urge is not the kind of effect we are most concerned with. Folks do all kinds of things with urges, many of which don't disrupt their lives at all. The kinds of effects we are concerned with are the ones that have real costs in people's lives. We are concerned with the urges you respond to in a way that limits your life. We are especially concerned with those responses that might move you away from a valued life.

We encourage you to practice noticing pulls in your life at least a few times. These won't show up as urges to erase anything. You won't have your list of "I am's" and "I am not's." But you *will* be carrying them with you. You didn't have to ponder anything or observe yourself over a long time to begin creating statements from your stories. And that's because they are always present. So we encourage you to practice noticing your stories and pulls in different places you go, during different activities you do.

When you run out on a short errand, set your watch or phone to beep every ten minutes, and when it does, pause and notice what stories might be pulling you around. Are you letting yourself off the hook once more because you are *just lazy?* Do you find yourself ignoring a friend's critical feedback because you know you are *a good friend?* Are you running late because you are *a person who never leaves a dirty dish in the sink?* Are you ignoring your friends altogether because you are busy *being beautiful* or *not being fat?*

VALUED PRACTICE

If you think it might be useful to you, we invite you to make a specific commitment to apply this practice to your values. Pause, take a few deep breaths, and think of at least one situation in your life in which opportunities for valued living might come up. It can be the same situation or situations you used in the last chapter, or you can pick another one. These would be situations in which there is something important to you at stake, but it would be easy to miss if you were stuck struggling with your story. For example, you might value being a sister and wish you could spend time with your sister without agonizing over how heavy you look. You might value your education and wish you could engage in class instead of fighting with all the ways you don't belong. Once you have a situation selected, call it to mind. Now imagine yourself in that situation, and watch yourself as you move through your world. What story is showing up? What do you do when it pulls?

Allow yourself to breathe the scene in and out three times, then write yourself a commitment below. For example, if you were the sister above, you might commit to scheduling regular time doing something together that you both enjoy, practicing your present-moment focus, and noticing when your desire to be thinner begins to come between you. Try to pick something that's doable, but still a challenge, and related to the value you chose in chapter 3. Don't rush this process of choosing your commitment. And remember, when you turn away from your commitment, the next thing to do is simply turn back.

In service of my value of _____ , I commit to the

practice of noticing my stories in the present moment by _____

_____

_____

_____

_____

Use the chart below to record your progress. There is space for five practice sessions. We suggest you do at least three. We also ask you to give yourself permission to hang out here with this commitment for a while, not moving forward in this work until you feel that you've begun to satisfy your commitment to yourself and are ready to move on.

The Mindfulness & Acceptance Workbook for Bulimia

66

	(Check below when complete)	Comments (for example, stories I noticed, effects they had)
Session 1		
Session 2		
Session 3		
Session 4		
Session 5		

MORE THAN A STORY: SELF-AS-CONTEXT

If you've spent some time as you move through this chapter watching these stories show up and pull you around, it's tempting to try to do something about them. If you're like most people, it doesn't take long before you start considering trying to forget some of those old stories, or rewrite them, or trade them in for new ones, or burn the books they're printed in. If you're like most people, you've noticed by now that we do not seem to be heading in that direction.

We started this chapter off by introducing the idea that knowing oneself has some virtue or benefit. And we're not quite ready to abandon that idea. The problem is that all too often, we work toward knowing the story. And when that story doesn't work, we seek out another. And another. And another. But what if it's not knowing the story that matters? People don't travel to China to "find themselves" because there is some information they forgot.

What if it's not the knowing at all, but noticing that matters? Noticing the story in the moments it starts to rise up... noticing what it feels like when it starts to take hold... noticing the ways your behavior changes as the pulls set in... Maybe the Greeks were just a little off. Maybe it's not *knowing* the self that matters, but *noticing* the self. Maybe having a new backdrop, or a new job, or a new look, or a new lover is about noticing the self amid the chaos of everything else.

Noticing Self

People often talk about "the self" as if it exists on some other plane—as if on some spiritual or mental level, this thing develops over time that is separate from our bodies but is, somehow, *us*. In ACT, we talk about the self a little differently. Just as we look at the context in which someone would learn to check channel 42, or pat a baby, or avoid bad feelings about her body, we look at the context in which someone would develop a sense of self.

BUILDING SELF, WRITING STORIES

B. F. Skinner was the first guy to talk about it this way, and he described it like this: From the moment we're born, everyone around us talks to us. They describe the world. They read us poems. They ask us questions. And pretty soon after we are born, we start responding. Some responses work out better than others. When we make sounds that are like talking, our parents cheer, and nuzzle us, and give us more attention. And we do more of that. And as we get older, it's not just any talking that works. Certain words we say in response to certain questions make our parents cheer, and nuzzle us, and give us more attention. "Who's that?... Mommy! Right!" Answering those questions involves us noticing certain experiences we are having. When we answer, "Mommy," we notice "who's that," and a finger pointing, and the woman it is pointing at. What if the self is like that? Many of the questions we are asked are about parts of our experience that others don't have access to. We're asked about physical sensations, thoughts, feelings, memories, and desires. "Are you cold?" "Are you hungry?" "What do you see?" "Do you want the blue one?" "What happened here?" "Why are you crying?" "What were you thinking?" The thing that is common to all of these questions is that they require us to recognize our own perspective, our *self*.

In ACT, we apply this idea to the ways that our stories about ourselves come to limit our lives. In the instant we recognize the self as distinct from the rest of the world, we begin to learn ideas *about* "the self" from others. We learn quickly that some things we do mean that we *are* "bad," and others mean that we *are* "good." We can learn that some things we do mean that we *are* "big kids" and that being "a big kid" is "good." We can learn that we *are* "cute," "beautiful," or "a little heavy." We can learn that we *are* "aggravating," "immature," or "a problem." And it's typically pretty clear whether what we *are* is okay or not. Even as adults we are bombarded every day with ideas about what we *are* and what we *should* be. And ACT suggests that the ones that seem most important to getting the cheers and the nuzzles and the attention from the folks around us, whether good or bad, are the ones that stay important later. These are the experiences that become the stories we carry around with us. These are the stories that are rich with pulls. These are the stories that tend to limit our lives.

SELF-AS-CONTEXT

In most cases, when we experience ourselves, we stay among the stories. Even when observing our appearance or behavior directly, it's all filtered through these stories about who we are and what that means. It is possible, however, to experience the self apart from any one story. It is possible to notice the self as the perspective from which each story emerges. It's the part of you that has been present in every moment from the moment you recognized that there was a *you*. It's the part of you that's been constant through every fear, every hope, and every disappointment. It's the part of you that was there before you knew all the things you know now. It's the part of you that was there when you wanted things you'd never want now. It's the part of you that was there when you believed in things you'd toss away now. It's the part of you that is neither good, nor bad, but has stories of both. It's the part of you that is not limited by any story of who you are, what you've done, or what you're capable of. It's a context from which anything could unfold.

From the first page of this book, we've been asking you to "notice this" or "notice that." We've been having you notice your breath. We've asked you to notice your thoughts and your feelings. In this chapter, we've had you notice your stories about yourself. We've asked you to notice the pulls that come with them. And now, we've hinted at noticing self. What we ask of you now is to notice the part of you that has been doing all that noticing. This is the part of you that can notice your breath, and your thoughts, and your feelings—the part of you that notices when you are or are not noticing them.

Noticing the self is not something that is particularly easy to talk about. It is, however, relatively simple to practice. One way to practice noticing the self is to take on a familiar mental job and then notice the part of you that is doing that job. In this practice, we're going to ask you to notice yourself noticing.

PRACTICE: NOTICING YOU NOTICING (GUIDED MEDITATION)

■ Set your timer for ten minutes. Pick something specific to focus on noticing for this practice. Think back to the last chapter, when you practiced applying present-moment focus to different parts of your experience (such as your breath, things you hear, things you feel in your body). Pick something that was easy for you to settle into noticing. If you need to, look back at the comments you recorded to help you select something. From now on, we'll call this your *lighthouse*.

■ When you're ready, start your timer and settle into a slow, steady pattern of breathing. When you notice yourself getting swept up into your thoughts about how you are breathing, what you've got going on in your life, or what you are about to do, simply turn your attention back to your breath and its gentle rhythm.

■ When you notice yourself settled in to your breath, gently shift your attention to the lighthouse you selected. See if you can't focus your attention completely on your lighthouse, letting the rest of your world fade. When you notice yourself distracted by other parts of your experience, shift your attention gently back to your lighthouse. And breathe.

▪ See if you can't trace the edges of your lighthouse in your mind. Notice where it begins in the whole of your experience. Notice all of the spaces in your experience where your lighthouse is not. Notice your lighthouse as just a tiny piece of everything that is making up your experience in this moment. And breathe.

▪ Notice who is noticing all of this—who becomes distracted and notices distraction. And breathe. Notice the infinite space through which your moment-to-moment experience flows. And breathe. When you find yourself lost in figuring this out or getting it right, let those experiences melt into the rest of your experience, and gently return first to noticing your lighthouse, then to noticing the you that is noticing. And breathe.

▪ When your timer sounds, gently let go of your focus, take three deep breaths, and open your eyes.

If you found yourself returning to your lighthouse again and again to start over, good. That's the nature of this practice. If you noticed yourself noticing only once or twice, and the experience didn't last long, congratulations. You did better than most people do when they practice this for the first time. If you found this confusing or frustrating, then that means you really made an effort.

Remember, the goal of this kind of practice would not be that you could just sit around noticing self-as-context without distraction forever. The goal is to be able to shift your attention to self-as-context in the moments when you notice those pulls yanking you in this direction or that. In that moment of being stuck, your awareness could grow to encompass not only what you were noticing, and that you were noticing, but also the you who was doing the noticing. And as your awareness spread, the possibilities for that next moment of action could spread with it.

Noticing Self as Valued Living

We said earlier that all this "self" stuff matters because of the way our stories about ourselves can limit the opportunities we see to take valued actions. If you don't see yourself as very smart or very strong or very beautiful, you might miss opportunities to be those things in a way that would serve your values. What if, when your pulls came up, you could notice yourself as more than some old story? What if, from that place, you could notice not only the pulls but the opportunities they hide? What if, from there, you could freely choose your next step? In some cases, you would choose to follow the pull, to take the next step in the story. In other cases, however, you would notice how that next step in your story would take you further from valued living. And without that story having to go away or change, you could step out of it and onto a path of your choosing.

VALUED PRACTICE

We encourage you to take just a moment here and notice how your stories and your values interact in the here and now.

- Call to mind the value you chose in chapter 2. And breathe. As you breathe, call to mind the situations you've selected for the other practices so far—situations connected to the things you really care about.

- Really see yourself in these situations. Watch yourself respond to the ongoing flow of experience, moving about your world. And breathe.

- When you feel present to your values, and to how valued living works in your day-to-day life, take a deep breath and imagine that something extraordinary could happen in this area of your life—something amazing that you wouldn't dare to hope for given the way things are now.

- See yourself experiencing that extraordinary change. Watch yourself in the moment you realized that something was different. Slow the scene down. What do you notice first? Watch your face change. What do you do next? And breathe.

- Notice any objections that your mind presents as to the possibility of this extraordinary thing occurring. Notice how they resonate or add to your stories. See if you can't breathe them in and out, still watching that extraordinary thing occur as the pulls strengthen. And breathe.

- When you notice yourself engaging the stories, thinking something like "it could happen," or "this sucks," or "why am I even trying," we encourage you to let go of that struggle. Take a deep breath and locate yourself as the space within which the imagined extraordinary happening, the objections to that imagination, and noticing of those takes place. See if you can't come to rest there, if only for a moment. And breathe.

If you think it might be useful to you, make a specific commitment to continue to apply this practice to your values. Look back at the situation you used for your commitment to noticing stories. Allow yourself to breathe the scene in and out three times, then write yourself a commitment below. For example, if you last committed to noticing stories about your weight while enjoying time with your sister, you might commit to noticing your self-as-context in those moments. Record your commitment below:

In service of my value of _____ , I commit to the practice

of noticing self-as-context in the present moment by _____

_____

_____

_____

Use this chart to record your progress. There is space for five practice sessions. We suggest you do at least three. We also ask you to give yourself permission to hang out here with this commitment for a while, not moving forward in this work until you feel that you've begun to satisfy your commitment to yourself and are ready to move on.

	(Check below when complete)	Comments (for example, effect of noticing self-as-context, challenges that came up)
Session 1		
Session 2		
Session 3		
Session 4		
Session 5		

So far, we've discussed two aspects of psychological flexibility: being present and self-as-context. These focus on practicing being fully present to both the ongoing experience and the perspective from which we experience. This "showing up" is the basis for the rest of the work we have before us. Call to mind the value you chose in chapter 2. How is the work you're doing with this book serving that value? Look back at the commitments you've made. Is there something different you could be doing with it that would serve that value? What is stopping you? If you find yourself struggling with these questions, take a couple of slow, deep breaths and let them drift from you. If it would be useful to you to go back and repeat some of your practices, please do so. This is *your* work, and you'll get the most out of it if you choose to engage in it in a way that works for *you*.

CHAPTER 5

A Great Big World: Looking Past Your Thoughts

Call to mind the last time you just *knew* somebody was wrong. Maybe you were arguing with a friend. Maybe you were watching political propaganda on Youtube. Maybe you were listening to some teenagers chatter on the bus. Maybe you had to resist the urge to shout from the mountaintops how this was just plain *wrong*.

Go ahead and take a deep breath and call to mind just one of these times. It doesn't have to be a particularly significant example—just one you can remember well enough to call up a few details. Let the scene play in your head for a moment or two. See if you can't recall your experience from the moment when you first thought "this is *not* right" to the end of the experience. What was it like for you? How aware were you of what was going on around you? How aware were you of what was going on within you?

For most people, an experience like this feels pretty overwhelming. Often people describe increasing discomfort, from the first moment to the last. Their bodies tense up. Their minds race. They often feel frustration or anger or disgust or sadness. And often they are bombarded by the urge to do something, anything, to make this all go away, but they seem unable to let it go.

FUSION: WHEN THOUGHTS TAKE OVER

In ACT, experiences like this are called *fusion*. By "fusion," we mean that certain thoughts (and feelings that come with them) take over your experience. You lose contact with most of what's going on within you and around you, except that thought you are fused with.

It's sort of like this. Take a deep breath and notice all of the things happening in this moment. Notice the world as it is right now. Now pick this book up and hold it flat against your forehead and your nose. Now notice the world as it is right now. It's pretty hard to notice anything but a book in your face. You can't even notice much about the book except that it seems sort of dark and maybe feels sort of smooth. Sometimes our thoughts are like this, right up against us, taking up most of our world. This is what we mean by "fusion."

Sense-Making, Action-Taking

Fusion is not without a purpose. As the world changes, our minds try their best to make sense of it. *What is that noise? Why is traffic stopping? What time is it? How long might this last?* And right up behind the thoughts that are about making sense are the thoughts about taking action. *What can I do about this?*

Often this "think, then do" stuff works out pretty well. We have thoughts, we take action, and the thoughts go away. In fact, part of what keeps things working like this is the awesome relief that comes as a consequence. Even with little things. You notice the dryer stops running when you just put something in. You think "I need to turn on the dryer" and you go over and start the cycle. Job done. Thoughts go away. "I'm glad I thought about it," you think, "my work pants were in there!"

But not every thought points to a dial to turn or a button to press. We can think about some things all day and never come up with anything to *do* that makes the thoughts go away. The problem is that we act as though all thoughts work the same way—as though there is always something to be done about them. And when it doesn't work out, we often have a hard time letting go.

The Thoughts to Nowhere

Ideally the thoughts we got most fused with would be the ones that pointed most clearly to action. Some thoughts are like this. We think, "I can't let that car hit my dog!" The rest of the world goes away for a minute and we run out to signal the car to stop. We think, "I have to go home and turn off the oven!" And we agonize the whole way home as we rush to turn off the oven.

But we get fused with thoughts all the time that feel like emergency action is required but that don't tell us what to do in any way that is meaningful or helpful. "He can't just *not call!*" And our world is dominated by that same tension, that same urge to act. Only there's nowhere to go with it, nothing to do. Not that that stops us. We do all kinds of things. We try to figure out why he's not calling. We think up an excuse to call casually. We tell him in no uncertain terms what we think of him. We try to forget that we ever cared. Often we rush through a flurry of things—mostly to make those thoughts, and the horrible feelings that come with them, go away.

TOO CLOSE TO NOTICE

"So," you might be thinking, "what is the alternative? How can I stop thinking?" Well, you can't. It's one of those things about being human. Our thoughts just kind of run in the background until the moment that they take over. And whether they are running in the background or mashing us in the face, we typically don't do a very good job of noticing that they are there. This lack of noticing, in fact, seems to be the start of the problem.

How do we do that? Well, suppose you saw someone sitting there with a book mashed up against her face. You approach her and ask what's up. She says, "I'm trying to check out this book. I thought it might be useful to me, but I'm having trouble. It's all dark in here. I'm not really getting much out of it." What might you do to help her out? Well, after you decided she wasn't dangerous, just very confused, you might suggest she pull the book out in front of her, where she could get a better look at it. You wouldn't insist she throw the book out, return it for a new one, or take up television. You'd see that the book wasn't the problem. It was how she was using the book, her relationship to it.

Noticing Thoughts

And it's the same with our thoughts. It's not that there's anything wrong with the thoughts themselves. Thinking helps us accomplish all kinds of things. It's not even what the thoughts say that matters. It's how we use our thoughts, our relationship to them.

We've given you a lot of explaining so far. And unfortunately, a lot of this is not easy to talk about. In this next practice, we'll ask you to take a few moments to practice noticing your thoughts. Almost like selecting books off the shelves of your memory, you'll call to mind several different images, one at a time. Your only job is simply to notice the thoughts that come up, in the same way you've practiced noticing the sensation of breathing.

PRACTICE: NOTICING THOUGHTS (GUIDED MEDITATION)

- Let your eyes close and take a few slow, deep breaths.

- Take a moment to notice what it feels like to take the air into your body. And to release.

- Call to mind the face of someone you like who you've seen recently. See if you can picture every element of his or her face, either as you last saw them, or as you imagine they look.

- As you imagine this person's face, notice any thoughts that come up. Notice the thoughts about the person whose face you're imagining—how much you like her, what you last did together, whether his eyes are brown or green. Notice thoughts that are completely unrelated—whether or not you remembered your lunch, how your back hurts, what your roommate said this morning. And breathe.

- And now, gently let that image pass as you take a slow, deep breath, noticing that familiar feeling of drawing air in and out.

- Call to mind the face of your mother or another female caregiver. See her eyes, her hair, her cheeks, her lips, her chin. See one of her familiar expressions as you remember it.

- And as you imagine her face, take a few moments to notice the thoughts that pass through your mind.

- Gently let that image pass as you take a slow, deep breath, noticing that familiar feeling of drawing air in and out.

- Call to mind now a place where at some time in your life you felt very safe and at home. Maybe it's a place in which you seek comfort now. Maybe it's somewhere you haven't been in a long, long time. It doesn't have to be a specific physical place. Maybe for you, comfort comes when you're doing a certain thing or spending time with a certain person. Without fretting too much over what exactly you pick, see yourself there, in that safe, comfortable place. Pick something specific that you can imagine in detail. And breathe.

- And as you imagine yourself there, take a few moments to notice the thoughts that pass through your mind.

- Gently let that image pass as you take a slow, deep breath, noticing that familiar feeling of drawing air in and out.

- Call to mind a moment in your life when you were very unhappy. See yourself in a moment when you were filled with despair or anger or frustration. See the expression on your face; see the way you moved. Hear your voice, if you spoke.

- And as you imagine yourself in that painful place, take a few moments to notice the thoughts that pass through your mind.

- Gently let that image pass as you take three slow, deep breaths, noticing that familiar feeling of drawing air in and out.

- Whenever you're ready, open your eyes.

One of the things you may have noticed in this practice is that noticing thoughts is another one of those things that is simple but not easy. Most people have to practice a bit before they even notice they're thinking at all. This usually feels awkward at first. We get all settled in and ready to notice, and it's almost like no thoughts come. Of course, thoughts come, but then we are so engaged in them that we forget to notice that we're thinking. It might be something like, "Okay... I'm ready to notice my thoughts... Come on, thoughts... Any time now..." Eventually, we learn to sort of catch ourselves thinking. It comes in little bursts of awareness (something like, "Oh wait! I guess I *am* thinking. Thinking that I'm thinking? Wait...") and then it's gone. Finally, we learn to observe our thinking without interrupting the process.

You also might have noticed that some thoughts are harder to observe than others. The ones that are hardest to observe are—you guessed it—the ones with which we are most fused. These are the massive ones we're mashed so completely against that we can't even see that they have edges. So if you really struggled with this practice, it may be beneficial to sit with it a little longer, noticing where you had the most trouble.

Which thoughts were more difficult for you to notice? Did you feel compelled to act on any of the thoughts you did notice? What was it like to let go of your thoughts when it was time to move on? Did any of this feel familiar to you? Record some of your experiences in the space below:

_____

_____

_____

_____

_____

_____

_____

There are other ways to practice noticing thoughts. Some people find visualization quite helpful. By imagining the thoughts you are having as though they were objects passing by, you can then imagine physical distance coming between you and those thoughts. The following is an example of that kind of practice.

PRACTICE: THOUGHTS ON PARADE
(GUIDED MEDITATION)

■ Set your timer for five minutes. Let your eyes close, and take three slow, deep breaths.

■ Start out by imagining that you are beside a street you know well. It should be a street you've stood and faced before. It can be in front of your house, outside of your work, downtown in your childhood—a street you could call up in detail, from the buildings around you to the street itself. And breathe.

■ Imagine that you are standing on this street when suddenly you realize a parade is moving down the street toward where you are standing. "A parade?" you might have just thought. If so, imagine those words on the banner at the front of the parade, question mark and all.

■ Breathe in, and as you release that breath, imagine that the banner passes you by.

■ For the next thought you notice, imagine it on another part of the parade—a float, a band, a pageant queen on the back of a convertible. Choose whatever feels most appropriate for that thought.

■ Breathe in, and as you release that breath, imagine that the next parade float passes you by.

■ Continue imagining your thoughts as part of this parade, one by one. And when you notice yourself distracted from the practice, put that distraction on a float or the logo of a marching band before moving on.

■ When your timer signals the end of five minutes, take one last deep breath and open your eyes.

Of course, a parade won't work for everyone. Some people enjoy picking a more peaceful scene that applies the same idea, such as imagining thoughts on leaves drifting down a stream. Some people get more out of imagining a very familiar image, such as putting thoughts on billboards they pass on the highway. Others do better if they imagine an active task, such as putting thoughts on pieces of laundry they are folding. We encourage you to try a couple of times, with a couple of different scenes.

And some folks don't find visualization helpful at all. If you find yourself fighting with visualizing rather than working on noticing thoughts, you might try using objects in your surroundings. For example, on your way to work, you could commit to notice what you're thinking each time you pass a traffic light.

Noticing Thoughts as Valued Living

Fusion matters most when it interferes with valued living. Unfortunately, this is not a rare occurrence. In fact, some of the thoughts we are most likely to fuse with are those that are somehow linked to our values. People will often justify fusion with these thoughts, saying, "Of course I'm not letting it go! It's important to me!" Often a thought like this seems to have a specific action attached to it. "I *have to* finish this by tomorrow. I just have to." And our world is dominated with the thought, and the tension, and the urge to act, and the thing to do is finish the project. And the more we care about this, and the more important it feels, the more fused we are.

Except the fusion can actually keep us from being able to work effectively. So we keep thinking, "I *have to* finish." And we keep not finishing. And we keep thinking, "I *have to* finish." And somehow having that thought, no matter how many times it comes up, or how intense the feelings are that come with it, doesn't help us get any closer to finishing. In fact, it typically moves us further from that goal. And this is why fusion matters to us at all. Because it's hard to head toward the things you care about with a book in your face!

VALUED PRACTICE

If you think it might be useful to you, we invite you to make a specific commitment to apply this practice of noticing thoughts to your values. Pause, take a few deep breaths, and think of at least one situation in your life in which opportunities for valued living might come up. It can be the same situation or situations you used in the previous chapters, or you can pick another one. This should be a situation in which there is something important to you at stake, but you wonder if your thoughts might be getting in the way of the parts of it that really matter to you. For example, you might value your relationship with your partner, and yet you notice you're always so ready to place blame when you feel hurt. You might value your work and wish you would take more opportunities to learn something new. Once you have a situation selected, call it to mind. Now imagine yourself in that situation and watch yourself as you move through your world.

Allow yourself to breathe the scene in and out three times, then write yourself a commitment below. For example, if you were the worker above, you might commit to learning one new thing a day, noticing the thoughts that come up as you do that. Try to pick something that's doable, but still a challenge, and related to the value you chose in chapter 2. Don't rush this process of choosing your commitment. And remember, when you turn away from your commitment, the next thing to do is simply turn back.

In service of my value of _____, I commit to practicing noticing

my thoughts in the present moment as I _____

_____

_____

Use the chart below to record your progress. There is space for five practice sessions. We suggest you do at least three. Practice in your life is what matters most here, and you'll use the things that you notice throughout the rest of this chapter.

	(Check below when complete)	Comments (for example, thoughts I noticed, effects they had)
Session 1		
Session 2		
Session 3		
Session 4		
Session 5		

RULES WE SUFFER BY

One of the things you may have noticed in the last practice is that some of the thoughts you noticed from session to session were not all that different. See, when it comes to our values, most of us get fused with the same sorts of thoughts over and over. Often, if we look a bit more closely, what we see underlying those thoughts are beliefs about what we have to do to live out our values. We value education, and we think, "Good students give right answers." We value our relationships, but "being too dependent on a partner will make them feel burdened."

Noticing Rules

Just as with our moment-to-moment thoughts, there's nothing wrong with the beliefs themselves. In fact, they are often the kinds of beliefs most people would agree with. The problems crop up because we treat these as if they are rules. And when we humans have a rule about what to do, it becomes the most important thing in the world in that moment. We miss signals in the world that would tell us what to do next. We miss opportunities in the world to take a valued step.

What if you're so caught up with having to know that you're right that you never risk looking wrong by participating in class? What are you willing to give up to be right? What if you're so stuck on not being dependent that you miss opportunities to help your partner feel needed and loved? What are you willing to give up to be independent?

VALUED PRACTICE
(GUIDED MEDITATION)

▦ Call to mind the value you've committed to doing this work for. Let your mind roll over the valued practices you've already done. Notice the thoughts that come up. And breathe.

▦ In the space below, jot down a few adjectives—as many as you like—that describe who you want to be with respect to that value. For example, you might value your health and write that you'd like to be "healthy," "energized," and "fit." You might value your relationship with your partner and write that you'd like to be "accepting" and "giving."

_____

_____

_____

▦ Look over these adjectives once or twice, breathing deeply and noticing any thoughts that come up as you read them. And breathe.

▦ Read these adjectives aloud, saying "I am…" before each of them. For example, if you wrote "healthy," "energized," and "fit," you'd say, "I am healthy. I am energized. I am fit." And breathe.

▦ Let your eyes close as you repeat these statements three to five times. Notice any urges to rush through this part or skip it. Notice the thoughts that come up as you state these things. And breathe.

▦ With your eyes still closed, slowly, gently take a moment to notice any rules that are showing up about what you'd have to do to be these things. Use these rules to complete the sentences below:

   ▦ If I ever want to be _____, I'll have to _____

   _____

   ▦ In order to be _____, I should _____

   _____

   ▦ Being _____ means I can't ever _____

   _____

▦ Now let your eyes close once more. Take three slow, deep breaths, noticing the thoughts swirling around you.

▦ Whenever you're ready, open your eyes.

Take a look at the sentences above. What's it like for you to read over these? How much possibility do you feel? How much hope? How much life? How about when these show up out there in your life when you're in a situation that matters to you? How easy is it for you to continue working toward your values? Is that opportunity part of what goes away as fusion sets in?

Rules That Don't Rule

Just like with any thoughts we have, rules are only one part of our experience at any one moment. And there's nothing in them that sets them apart from any other thought. It's all in the way we relate to them. It's like sometimes we get into situations where having the book in our face sort of shields us from scary stuff, so we pick it up over and over. In other words, they are *rules* only because we *let them rule*.

What would it be like to notice your rules when they come up, without them taking over? You could feel uneasy in class, think about what that seems to say about you, and still see the chance to participate. You could feel needy and weak, think about what that seems to say about you, and still see the chance to reach out. In ACT, this is called "defusion." As you might guess, defusion simply refers to experiencing without any one thought taking over.

Loosening the control rules have over our behavior takes practice. How do we practice defusion? We practice calling to mind our rules, then doing anything other than following them. Not because they are wrong—it's important to do things right and be independent and not hurt people—but because we already know how to follow rules. We don't need any practice at fusion.

We've already practiced this a couple of times. Noticing is different from following, so practicing noticing thoughts (rules included) is one way to practice defusion. This is invaluable because in any moment, in any situation, you can pause, take a deep breath, and notice your thoughts. Sometimes it's beneficial to use language to help you notice your thoughts. Saying something like, "You know, I keep having this thought that I'm going to feel sad like this forever" feels very different from saying "I'm going to feel sad like this forever."

BEYOND NOTICING

Defusion is not just about noticing. There are tons of ways to relate to your thoughts that don't involve letting them control what you do. Bringing up your rules on purpose and being playful with them can help you to change your reaction when they show up without your permission. Below are a few ideas.

PRACTICE: LOST IN SENSATION

Some defusion practices focus on writing down or speaking part of the rule, then paying close attention to the raw sensation of what it looks, feels, or sounds like:

- Say the rule as slowly as you possibly can (for example, "IIIIIIIIIIIIIIIIIIII haaaaaaaaaaavvve tooooooooooooo beeeeeeeeeee strooooooooooooooong."), noticing the sounds of each phoneme.

- Say the rule as slowly as you possibly can, noticing the way it feels in your mouth and throat.

- Write the rule on every line of a piece of looseleaf, using a different color ink for every word. When you finish, hold the paper out in front of you and notice the patterns it makes.

- Type the rule in a word processing program. Change the font size to 72, and zoom 500 percent. Notice the shapes the letters make on the page.

- Write an important word from your rule across the middle of a piece of paper in cursive. Underline it, then trace the word on the other side of the same line, allowing the tails to overlap the other word. Flip the page so the line is vertical. Get out your art supplies and see what you can do with the shapes.

- Repeat the rule, starting off slowly, then gradually speeding up until you're saying it as fast as you can. Notice the way the words blend into one another.

PRACTICE: DEFUSION THEATRE

Some defusion practices focus on saying the rule as if the words had completely different meanings. Grab a mirror and try a few of these as you read along:

- Pick your favorite showtune and sing your rule. (Dance, for extra effect.)

- Say your rule as if it were a cheesy pickup line.

- Explain your rule in great detail, as if you were a professor giving a lecture on being the perfect you.

- Deliver your rule as if it were an infomercial.

- Say your rule with a thick accent.

- Say your rule in the voice of your favorite cartoon character.

- Offer your rule as if it were a dramatic sermon.

PRACTICE: GO PUBLIC

Some defusion practices focus on sharing the rule with other people without explaining anything about what you're doing:

- ▓ Design a T-shirt, mug, or other custom product sporting your rule. If you are really bold, create and use it. (There are tons of websites that offer custom products if you're not artistically inclined.)

- ▓ Design and print temporary tattoos for wearing your rule on the days it shows up the worst. (Again, this is easy online.)

- ▓ Walk up and shake a stranger's hand, telling them your rule as if you were introducing yourself.

- ▓ Post your rule as your status on your favorite social networking site.

- ▓ Write your rule on a nametag and wear it on an errand.

- ▓ Drive down a lonely road, yelling your rule out of the window.

- ▓ Make a postcard from your rule and submit it to postsecret.com.

We encourage you to try at least a few of these defusion practices and to make up at least one of your own. Check off the practices you try. If you're having the thought that all of this sounds hard or time-consuming, or a little silly, notice that. And ask yourself if the value you chose isn't worth the extra time or effort or embarrassment.

FUSION AND THE STRUGGLE WITH EATING

Fusion can play an important role in maintaining eating struggles. It often goes something like this: You're eating without much struggle about how much or when or in front of whom. Then a hard thought comes up and takes over your world. It might be an evaluation of your appearance ("fat-ass"), a physical sensation ("stuffed"), or something you eat ("disgusting"). And you begin restricting. But that doesn't make the hard thought go away. In fact, it might bring new hard thoughts with it ("out of control," "weak," "messed up"). Again, your world is swallowed up. So you let go of restricting and overeat. But the hard thoughts get worse, so you compensate. But that comes with its own hard thoughts. So you begin restricting again. And so you find yourself fighting to eat in a way that manages your thoughts. Most people who struggle with eating have rules around beauty, sensations of fullness, and food.

Rules About Beauty

Sometimes, when beauty has been emphasized as an important part of a person's worth, he or she develops rules about both *what beauty means* and *what beauty is*. People who struggle with eating are often quite fused with their ideas about the worth of beauty. Often beauty is equated with confidence, power, and social acceptance. And when thoughts about being or not being confident, powerful, or accepted come up, very little else is as compelling as looking a certain way. That "certain way" is often "thin." Typically individuals who struggle with eating equate thinness with beauty. People may tend to focus on a particular body part such as the abdomen, the hips, or the legs, judging beauty only by the appearance of that one part. For example, a person might be normal weight but judge herself as overweight because her abdomen is not toned.

What rules do you have about beauty? What does being beautiful mean to you? How do you judge your own beauty? When do you feel most unattractive? What labels do you use to describe your body when you're feeling unattractive? What do you do about it? Jot down the rules about beauty that come to mind below:

_____

_____

_____

_____

_____

Rules About Feeling Full

People who struggle with eating often develop rules about *what fullness means* and *what fullness is*. Fullness is often equated with gluttony. When guilt and shame come up, everything except those thoughts and the fullness they're linked to goes away. This can be particularly dangerous when the threshold for what is *too full* becomes lower and lower. People can get to a point where even the smallest amount of food in the stomach is intolerable and distracts them from everything else in their world.

What rules do you have about fullness? How do you know when you are full? Where do you feel fullness in your body? What labels do you use to describe feeling full? What do you do about it? Jot down the rules about feeling full that come to mind below:

_____

_____

Rules About Food

People struggling with eating often develop rules about food. Foods are often sorted into rigid mental categories, such as "safe" and "guilt-free" or "dangerous" and "forbidden." This sorting is often based on very limited aspects of the food, like fat or carbohydrate content. It can also be based, however, on sensations like texture or taste, or even the way eating it makes the person feel or appear to others. In any case, it is often these "forbidden" foods that people choose to binge on. The unpleasant feelings that follow a binge serve to strengthen the idea that this food should be avoided.

What rules do you have about food? What foods do you avoid? What do they have in common? What labels do you use to describe foods you avoid? Jot down the rules about food that come to mind below:

_____

_____

_____

_____

Other Rules That Keep the Struggle Going

Because every person's history and environment is different, most people have other rules that seem related to their eating struggle. Take a moment and call to mind other rules that are part of your struggle with eating. Even if you've already worked with them in previous sections, record them below:

_____

_____

_____

_____

VALUED PRACTICE

If it feels useful to you, we invite you to apply the defusion you've practiced throughout this chapter specifically to your struggle with eating. Pause, take a few deep breaths, and think of at least one situation in your life in which your struggle with eating interferes directly with valued living. This should be a situation in which you have the opportunity to pursue something that really matters to you but your rules about beauty, feelings of fullness, and food get in the way. For example, you might recognize how you miss out on meaningful interactions with your romantic partner because of your fusion with thoughts of your appearance. Once you have a situation selected, call it to mind. Now imagine yourself in that situation, and watch yourself as you move through your world.

Allow yourself to breathe the scene in and out three times, then write yourself a commitment below to do one of the defusion techniques you've practiced with this rule. Continuing the example above, you might commit to wearing a nametag that says, "If I'm not beautiful, I'm nothing" when you're around your partner.

In service of my value of _____ , I commit to _____

_____

_____

_____

Now, we've discussed three aspects of psychological flexibility: being present, self-as-context, and defusion. These focus on being fully present to the ongoing experience and the perspective from which we experience, without any one aspect of our experience dominating. Let yourself notice the pieces of this work that you've integrated into your life, and notice the influence that has had. Notice the pieces you've practiced from safely behind the book. Notice the pieces you've skipped altogether. And breathe. In the next chapter, we'll explore the ways we hold ourselves back from some of our experiences, then explore what we can do differently.

CHAPTER 6

Embracing Experience:
Learning Acceptance

Since you opened this book, you've been spending time paying close attention to things you probably hadn't thought a whole lot about before. You've spent time noticing your ongoing experiences, noticing your perspective that's common to those experiences, and looking past difficult thoughts. It's likely that not all of this has been comfortable for you. In fact, some of what we've asked you to approach has probably been downright painful.

It's worth recognizing that we didn't introduce painful stuff into your world. We didn't tell you sad stories, call you names, let you down, or reveal some injustice you never knew about. We simply pointed to aspects of your life or your experience. And it doesn't do much to point to things that aren't present. In other words, this stuff, from the uncomfortable to the agonizing, is stuff that you walk around with every day. It's stuff that could show up in any moment.

So why doesn't it? Why is it that thoughts and feelings lying just under the surface feel so overwhelming when you notice them? ACT would suggest that there are painful things affecting us all the time. We just happen to be pretty good at turning away from them.

LEARNING TO TURN AWAY

In chapter 2, we presented the idea that the things we do are the things we've learned—that our behavior comes from its context. One thing that humans learn easily is to avoid hurt. This not only means avoiding food that makes us sick or objects that are hot. Humans can learn to avoid things that are right inside of our own experience. Thoughts and feelings. Memories. Images. Perceptions.

We can learn to avoid the thought that we might fail or the memory of a death in the same way that we learn not to touch boiling water. This avoidance is a bit more insidious, though. We don't carry boiling water with us. It's not likely that burning ourselves once would mean we never touch anything again. We do, however, carry our experiences with us. So we come across something that hurts in our lives. And we struggle for a while, doing anything that gives us relief. And it works. We can breathe for a second. But unlike boiling water, even as we avoid, we carry that hurt with us. And when it comes up again, we avoid again. And it works. Until it doesn't. And because of the way that our minds work, that hurt spreads until we have to work a little harder to get the same relief. And eventually, avoidance is not a discrete shift, like pulling your hand away before you get burned. It becomes a way of moving through the world.

It Takes a Village

One of the reasons why this work feels strange is because, for the most part, we tend to support each other in avoiding our own experiences. Much of our culture's media sends the message that if we are not happy, then something is wrong. If we feel lost or confused or alone, it's assumed that there's a problem. And often presented are two possibilities. Either the problem is in the things around us, and we need that car or that beer or that television to feel okay, or else the problem *is* us, and we need some medication to feel okay.

We propagate the idea that it's normal to be happy through our everyday interactions. When we see someone crying, we say, "What's *wrong?*" as if sadness is abnormal. We ask, "How's it going?" way more frequently than we actually expect to get a meaningful answer. What would it be like if one day we asked "What's up?" and a coworker replied, with tears in her eyes, "Things have been really hard lately. I'm just not sure what to do anymore." Even with the people closest to us, we can often find ourselves doing way more shushing and soothing than listening. Most days, we conspire with those around us to turn away from their experiences, all the while keeping lips sealed about our own.

Recognizing Avoidance

Because we all have our own histories and our own lives, it's not always easy to recognize avoidance. It's not the kind of behavior we can describe in terms of what it looks like, because it's defined by how it works. And the same behavior works different ways, depending on the context. Two people might be struggling with an unexpected breakup. One stays home and watches movies to avoid being reminded of the loss. The other makes big plans with close friends to avoid being reminded of the loss. Going out and staying home are similar in this example. They look much different, but they are both serving as avoidance. Not only that, but both staying home and going out could be done in a way that were not avoidant.

When some psychologists talk about avoidance, they are talking about behavior that can be seen from the outside. There are places we don't go because of the thoughts and feelings that show up in our experience when we're there. We all have things we do to avoid, however, that others can't see. We shove an idea out of our minds. We fantasize about other possibilities. We problem solve. We make plan A. We make plan B. We argue with ourselves. We "look on the bright side." We think about something else. We try to forget.

Noticing Avoidance

Even more challenging than characterizing a behavior as avoidant or not is noticing we are avoiding in the moment when it occurs. Much of our avoidance runs on autopilot. We don't have to know that we are avoiding, or even that we are hurting, for avoidance to occur. In other words, anything we do that lessens or delays or stops hurt is avoidance, whether or not we would describe it like that. We can, however, learn what avoidance feels like for us, and we can learn to notice it in the moment. One way to practice noticing avoidance is to pay attention to the moment just before we turn away from something hard, a practice we call listening for the "no."

PRACTICE: LISTENING FOR THE "NO" (GUIDED MEDITATION)

- Let your eyes gently close. Take three slow, deep breaths, noticing how it feels to pull the air into your body and to release it.

- Let your mind reach back to yesterday at the moment you first opened your eyes. See yourself there, and see the space around you. Let yourself breathe that moment in and out.

- When you feel settled into that moment, slowly begin to roll the day forward. Follow your flurry of activity from the moment you woke up yesterday until today. And breathe.

- If you find yourself struggling to keep things in order, or reaching to remember everything perfectly, pause and take a slow, deep breath. Let the memory come as it comes.

- Now, allow yourself to settle upon a single moment in the day yesterday when you felt a "no" rise up in your experience. It doesn't have to be a particularly important moment. It could just be an instant. Maybe someone said something that hurt you, or another driver cut you off in traffic, or you found yourself suddenly thinking of someone who's no longer around. Any moment when the world pushed on you in a way that felt not okay, and you pushed back. And breathe.

▪ Breathe that moment in and out. Notice the details of the space around you: Who was with you? What sounds or smells were in the air?

▪ See your face just before the hurt came, and the "no" right behind it. Notice the way you looked, sounded, and moved. Watch your eyes just before your experience shifted and began to sting.

▪ See if you can't pour yourself into that moment, seeing through yesterday's eyes, breathing yesterday's air. Hesitate there a moment, letting the world fill in around you as it was just then.

▪ Now, take one last breath there before allowing the events to roll slowly forward.

▪ Notice the instant the hurt first shows up. Where do you feel it in your body?

▪ See if you can't recognize the "no" just behind it. Notice how quickly it comes.

▪ Notice the experience behind the "no"—how the world feels different. And breathe.

▪ Watch yourself respond. What did you do next? How did you move through your world once that "no" was hanging around?

▪ See if you can notice how long the "no" hung around, how your behavior changed as it dissipated. And breathe.

▪ Take three slow, deep breaths, noticing the familiar feeling of your own breath, right now.

▪ Whenever you're ready, open your eyes.

What did "no" feel like for you? Was it a familiar feeling? How did your behavior change when you were avoiding? Jot down some of what you noticed below. Try not to get too caught up in explaining it just right or even making sense of it just yet. The important part now is to write down enough details that you could call the experience back up if you tried.

_____

_____

_____

_____

_____

_____

COSTS OF COMFORT

Chopping off little pieces of our experience, it seems, is not without cost. ACT is based on the idea that although we all do it, avoidance rarely works out for us. We are not only not very good at avoiding, but our efforts to avoid seem to be pretty toxic.

Don't Want It, You Got It

For one, we are not particularly effective at avoiding thoughts and feelings. In fact, it seems the more we try to manage these experiences, the more we are reminded of them.

PRACTICE: NOT THAT GUY AGAIN

- Call to mind someone who annoys you. If you can't think of someone right away, think of someone you found annoying in the past—someone you'd want to cross the street to avoid if you saw him or her walking toward you. Write that person's name here: _____

- Set your timer for two minutes.

- Start your timer. The only thing to do in this exercise is notice when you think of the person whose name you wrote above. Make a mark in the space below each time you think about him or her, however briefly.

- Now reset your timer, again for two minutes. This time, once you start the timer, all you need to do is try your absolute best to *not* think about the person whose name you wrote above. Make a mark in the space below each time you think about him or her, however briefly.

- Count your marks.

So, how successful were you at not thinking about *that guy*? Most people have to honestly respond, "not very." In fact, for most people, trying to keep a thought from coming up actually makes it come up more often. And for many, the more dangerous the thought feels and the more important it feels to suppress it, the more unsuccessful suppression is.

Of course, there are other ways of managing thoughts. Some therapies focus on getting control of thoughts in order to get control of feelings and behavior. New theories on how thoughts work suggest, however, that we can really only add to thinking patterns, not replace thoughts altogether. It may be that repeatedly attempting to change our thoughts not only isn't helpful, but can actually be toxic.

The Backward Compass

Another cost of avoidance is felt in the ways that it can disrupt our lives. We all come to places in our lives when we realize that we've been using our thoughts and feelings as a compass. If there are certain parts of our experience we can't have, then there are certain places we can't go—physically and psychologically. So when the hurt starts, we change direction. The problem is that our thoughts and feelings don't seem to be anything more than pieces of our history that we carry with us. How much are you willing to limit your life to avoid feeling sad? How about alone? How much would you give up to avoid feeling scared? To avoid feeling disappointed? Vulnerable? Regretful? How much would you be willing to squeeze your life down, knowing that you'd only have to sacrifice more as time went on?

The disruption doesn't stop at a little sacrifice every once in a while. Avoidance lies at the root of the struggles we typically think of as psychological problems or "mental disorders." What we call "depression" doesn't disrupt life because of sadness. It's when people start to tune out or go still to manage the sadness that they run into trouble. It's not being anxious that causes problems in people's lives—it's the act of managing anxiety by worrying or staying home. It's not even hallucinations or delusions that make psychosis so disruptive. It's the things people do in response to them. What if it's just not possible to turn away from things that hurt without turning away from whole chunks of our lives?

Values and Vulnerabilities

Finally, sometimes the pieces of our lives we turn away from to save ourselves from hurt are the ones that matter most to us. Right inside of the things we care about most are our greatest vulnerabilities. If we can't allow failure, we can't ever fully devote ourselves to something. If we can't stand rejection, we can't ever be known by another. If we can't abide loss, we can never possess. It's not that these things will necessarily come to pass, but certainly they will be present, if only in our fears.

Valued Practice

Even in committing to working toward a particular value, which you've done throughout this book, you've had to come up against hurt. And there were probably some moments when you turned away. You set the book down, went on to something else, tried not to think about the work you were doing here. And in another moment you turned back. Take a moment now and consider the vulnerabilities you reveal in committing to the value you've chosen to work toward in this book.

▪ Take three slow, deep breaths and let your eyes close.

▪ Call to mind the value that you've been working toward throughout this book. Take a moment to breathe your sense of what this value means to you in and out.

▪ Now allow yourself to see, one at a time, the specific situations in which you've practiced valued living. Watch yourself in the moments you stretched and built something new. Watch yourself in the moments you froze and turned away. Watch gently, as if you could offer yourself some support in those moments. And breathe.

▪ And as you watch yourself turn away and turn back in the places in your life that really matter to you, notice the edges between turning away and turning back. In the moments between them, notice the hurt that shows up. The fears, the regrets. And breathe.

▪ Notice the "no's" that rush in just behind the hurt. How they sweep your behavior away. Where they take it. What you might miss there. And breathe.

▪ See if you can't notice inside of those moments what vulnerabilities you uncover as you take steps toward your values. What vulnerabilities you are protecting when you turn away. And breathe.

▪ Without letting go of your sense of those vulnerabilities, take three slow, deep breaths, noticing the familiar feeling of drawing the air into your body and pushing it out.

▪ Whenever you're ready, open your eyes and, right away complete the statements below.

I value: _____

In valuing this, I risk: _____

_____

_____

_____

_____

I sometimes avoid exposing this vulnerability by: _____

_____

_____

_____

_____

For me, the cost of this avoidance is: _____

_____

_____

_____

_____

Look over your responses. If you find yourself wanting to look away, to move on, simply pause and notice that urge to turn away even now. Take three deep breaths. Ask yourself: *What are you willing to give up to avoid feeling those vulnerabilities? What are you willing to give up to avoid those hurts?*

AVOIDANCE AND THE STRUGGLE WITH EATING

Many people who struggle with eating describe a constant battle to eat differently—to eat less, to eat slowly, to eat often, to eat only organic food. And for most, this started out as eating in a way that brought them some relief from persistent struggles with body image. They don't like what they see in the mirror, what they feel as they move about their world, what they see in other people's eyes. And managing eating can be a way of doing something about these parts of their experience. In time, many start to apply this strategy to other parts of their experience that feel out of their control. In the moment that they are carefully restricting, they get some relief from the parts of life that cannot be controlled in this way. It's not sustainable, however. The concerns return, and eating patterns are often too rigid to continue long term.

For many of these same people, eating has also been a source of comfort. Maybe Mom offered a snack after a bike crash or stubbed toe. And when the picture tore, they asked for a snack. And when they didn't get invited to the party, they indulged. So when the hurt feelings, and the fears, and the regret they carry are weighing them down, eating shows up as a way to gain a little bit of relief. When restricting eating is no longer sustainable, binge eating becomes increasingly likely. Many describe "zoning out" while binge eating. Their struggle goes away for a moment. Again, they find some short-lived relief.

With this relief, however, comes a whole new host of hurts: guilt, disappointment, frustration, and disgust, along with the familiar body image concerns. At this point many return to restricting. And so the avoidance cycle maintains itself.

This next practice will involve calling to mind instances of avoidant eating in your own life and noticing the "no" that shows up even as you remember those experiences. This is likely to be a difficult practice. The more these eating struggles disrupt your life in valued areas, the more difficult this is likely to be.

PRACTICE: NOTICING AVOIDANT EATING

- Take three slow, deep breaths and let your eyes close.

- As you breathe, notice how it feels to pull the air in. And to release.

- Call to mind an instance when you were making a specific effort to control your eating. Maybe you counted calories carefully in your head. Maybe you denied yourself a certain treat you wanted. Maybe you made a point to leave a certain amount of food on your plate. Whatever form it took for you, let the scene appear before you. Notice where you were and who was there with you. Notice any smells or sounds on the air. Watch yourself as you navigated this specific act of eating. And breathe.

- Pay special attention to the places where your behavior went rigid, where it was inflexible. Notice the "no" that shows up there, that sense of desperation. That you *must* get through this. And breathe.

- Gently let that scene fade as you call to mind an instance in which you ate more than you'd intended, in which you felt that sense of control leave you. Notice where you were and who was there with you. Notice any smells or sounds on the air. And breathe.

- Notice when your focus shifts—from present to not—and the shift back to awareness. And breathe.

- Pay special attention to the places where your behavior went rigid, where it was inflexible. Notice the "no" that shows up there, that sense of desperation. That you *must* get through this. And breathe.

■ Gently let that scene fade as you call to mind an instance in which you were attempting to make up for having eaten more than you wanted to. Notice where you were. Notice any smells or sounds on the air. And breathe.

■ Notice when your focus shifts—from present to not—and the shift back to awareness. And breathe.

■ Pay special attention to the places where your behavior went rigid, where it was inflexible. Notice the "no" that shows up there, that sense of desperation. That you *must* get through this. And breathe.

■ Gently let that scene fade as you return your attention to the here and now.

■ Notice the "no" that shows up even now, that familiar sense of desperation. That you *must* get through this. And hesitate here for just a moment.

■ Take three slow, deep breaths, noticing how it feels to breathe in and out.

■ Whenever you're ready, open your eyes.

A part of you probably wants to shove that experience as far from your mind as possible. These are not experiences that most people like to think about—and that is just another layer of avoidance. We not only avoid body image concerns or fears of disappointment, but avoid our own avoidance. Take a moment and notice some of the thoughts or feelings you can't stand to have—both ones that showed up in the eating experiences and ones that showed up as you recalled the eating experiences. These are the experiences that you're likely to work to avoid. Record these below:

I avoid _____.

I avoid _____.

I avoid _____.

I avoid _____.

I avoid _____.

I avoid _____.

And now, take a moment to notice what avoidant eating looks like for you. How do you avoid the experiences you recorded above?

Examples of my avoidant eating include: _____

_____

_____

Take a moment to notice the costs that avoidant eating has in terms of your values.

My avoidant eating takes away from my valued living by:_____

_____

_____

_____

_____

_____

And now, take a deep breath and consider—what would it be like for you to come up against those hurts, those thoughts and feelings you can't stand, and to continue moving toward the things you care about?

SAYING "YES": ACCEPTANCE

For many people, it feels as though from the moment those "no's" first show up, their choices are limited. Most of the world disappears, and the only thing they are really aware of is the hurt and any way they can think of to get away from it. They find themselves stuck. Stuck in that moment with only one way out. Stuck in their lives with avoidant eating as the only way out. But what if there's more?

Finding Freedom

ACT rests on the assumption that there is certainly more. We're just letting our hurt tell us what to do and where to go. To look more closely at this, we'll use a version of the ACT metaphor of an uninvited guest (Hayes, Strosahl, and Wilson 1999).

THE UNINVITED

Imagine you're at a party and that guy has crashed it. (Remember? That annoying guy that you tried not to think of? *That guy.*) We're going to pretend it's a male, but apply this metaphor using the person you practiced with before). So you can't stand this guy. You're having a good ol' time—laughing with friends, meeting new people. And suddenly you hear the doorbell ring, the door open, and his voice carry from the foyer. "Oh no…" you think, "not here!" But he's still in the foyer, and you're in the living room, so you are able to sort of take a deep breath and keep talking.

As the conversation continues, you can hear him working his way into the room you're in. You find yourself scanning periodically to see where he is, listening for his voice, looking for his face. And every once in a while, he sneaks into your attention from the other room—a smirk or laugh suddenly distracting you from the conversation in front of you. Eventually, he makes his way into the living room.

Now, you really can't stand this guy, so you move on to the dining room. Same thing here—you're half-distracted, but sort of able to keep up with the conversation—until he enters the dining room. When you see him, you move on to the kitchen. And then he's in the kitchen, so you slip out back, and then he's there, so you walk around to the front. And so on, and so forth, all so you can keep this guy at bay, keep this annoyance under control.

Now at this point we ask you—who's in control? That guy's been roaming free all over the party, and you've been killing yourself trying to stay away. So who's in charge there? You? Or him?

How similar is this to the things we do to avoid hurt? The idea is to control our experience, to not let hurt overwhelm us and take control. But our usual response is to let that hurt dictate where we get to go. And just like *that guy*, the hurt isn't showing up with any rhyme or reason. Neither is there to improve our experience or to help us figure out what to do next. Yet by trying to control them, we are controlled by them. And in allowing them to control us, we miss opportunities to pursue the things we care about. The question has been phrased like this—*do you have hurt or does hurt have you?*

WELCOMING THE UNINVITED

So what would it be like to welcome *that guy* when he showed up? To acknowledge his presence there, at the party, and welcome him to stay as long as he liked? Does a "no" show up for you as you read this? As you imagine welcoming him? "Wait," you might be thinking, "if I welcome him, he'll stay!" Maybe. He was staying anyway, right? Notice that we are not proposing that you insist he be included when the guest list is made. Or that you clutch him about his knees when he tries to leave. We're also not convinced that that would make any difference to what he did. It would, however, mean that when he showed up, you got to stay. Not just that first time, but every time. That when you turned away from a conversation or an interaction, it would be a choice.

This work does not stop at just noticing the hurt, the "no," and our own avoidance. ACT is based on the idea that even when "no" is showing up everywhere we turn, we can still say "yes." And in that moment of "yes," our choices open up. In that moment, we are free.

PRACTICE: LETTING GO OF "NO"

■ Set your timer for ten minutes. Take three slow, deep breaths and let your eyes gently close.

- As you breathe, let yourself notice how it feels to draw the air into your body and to release it. Take several breaths to settle in here before moving on.

- See if you can't reach back in your mind to yesterday. Let yourself start by seeing the moment you woke up yesterday. Call to mind the details of that moment—where you were, the objects that were around you, who else was there with you. And breathe.

- Now take a minute to let the events of yesterday and today roll out before you. Try not to grasp too hard for events that slip from your memory. And breathe.

- It's not important that the memories come in a certain order. Just see if you can't slow down a bit inside these events as you let the memories sort of flow through you. And breathe.

- As you watch yourself in this single day, notice the places you go and don't go, the choices you make and the places your "no's" get in the way of choice. And breathe.

- Whenever you're ready, allow yourself to settle on a moment somewhere between yesterday and today in which you can feel a "no" rising up. It doesn't have to be a particularly important moment. It could just be an instant. Maybe someone said something that hurt you, or someone cut you off in traffic, or you found yourself suddenly thinking of someone who's no longer around. Any moment when the world pushed on you in a way that felt not okay. And you pushed back. And breathe.

- See if you can't pour yourself into your skin in that moment, looking out from your eyes, from inside that "no." Let the details of the world as it was in that moment fill in around you. Let the thoughts and feelings you had in that moment rise up inside you. And breathe.

- Now let your attention come to rest on the "no." Notice where you feel that "no" in your body right now, what it feels like, the shape it takes. Notice how tightly you're holding onto that "no," how firm your grip is. And breathe.

- Let yourself notice what's just on the other side of that "no," the hurt you are turning away from. What experience are you unwilling to have? What might you think, feel, or see if you let go of that "no?" What are you saying "no" to? And breathe.

- Imagine now that you loosened the grip that you have on that "no." Not to try to push it away or anything, just to free your hands and your attention for other things. What if you let that "no" go?

- Now take three slow, deep breaths, and as you exhale, imagine yourself gently, slowly letting go of this "no," letting go of your resistance against the hurt that shows up here more and more with each breath.

- See if you can't let the hurt you've been fighting fill you more and more with each breath. Notice where you feel that hurt in your body. How it pulls at you. The thoughts that come with it.

- And when you find yourself picking that "no" up once more, and holding it before you like a shield, take a slow, deep breath. As you exhale, let the "no" gently slip through your fingers once more. And when you feel the urge to pick it up again, remember it will still be there for you as soon as you're ready to pick it up again. And breathe.

■ Breathe the hurt in and out slowly. When you hear your timer, open your eyes.

Those moments when you felt your grip on that "no" loosen, when you opened yourself up to the hurt that was approaching, *that* is acceptance. If you found it hard to get there, you're not alone.

Acceptance is a lot easier to talk about than to do. But it turns out that talking about it doesn't do us much good. When we say we "accept" something out in the world, we often mean that either we like it as it is, or we've given up on it being any different. When we use "acceptance" as a technical term, we mean neither that we like what we are feeling nor that we are stuck there. Instead, we mean noticing how we're feeling, that we don't like it, and that we are not stuck anywhere. If you can think and feel anything that comes up, you can go anywhere.

Acceptance as Valued Living

Acceptance, in and of itself, is not particularly virtuous. Just because a behavior is avoidant doesn't mean that it's bad or that you should stop. Earlier in this chapter, however, you identified situations in which your avoidance interferes with your values. Acceptance is important only for the ways that it provides you with the freedom to live those values.

Look back at the work you did at the beginning of this chapter, considering the hurt you risk by caring about the things you value. One of the questions we asked was about the things you value that you give up to avoid that hurt. We ask that question now another way—what could you do that you value if you could embrace that hurt?

Valued Practice

Pause, take a few deep breaths, and call to mind a specific situation in which avoidance has interfered with valued living. Notice the way hurt has crept into that situation and how you've responded to it. For example, you might notice how struggling to not feel sad or angry when you're with people you care about just makes you more isolated. You might recognize how trying to avoid disappointment by putting less than full effort into things has only increased the likelihood of your disappointment. You might notice how fighting against self-doubt by holding back and playing small has kept you from really experiencing life. Make a few notes below that detail the kind of hurt that you avoid in this situation, what that avoidance looks like, and how it affects valued living:

_____

_____

_____

_____

Now, we invite you to make a specific commitment to embracing your experiences in this situation. For example, you might commit to welcoming feelings that come up when you're with people you care about and asking for support when you feel like you need it. You might commit to choosing to do at least one thing a week that you really doubt you can accomplish but that would be meaningful for you to go after anyway. Be as specific as you can, including details about what thoughts or feelings you think might come up, and when you think this might be important.

In service of my value of _____, I commit to accepting _____

_____ that comes up when _____

_____

_____

Use the chart below to record your progress. You know how it goes.

	(Check below when complete)	Comments (for example, thoughts I noticed, effects they had)
Session 1		
Session 2		
Session 3		
Session 4		
Session 5		

Now, we've discussed all four aspects of psychological flexibility that can help make possible our commitments to valued living: being present, noticing self-as-context, looking past fused thoughts, and accepting our experiences as they come. Our next piece of work is to prepare you to integrate these into your everyday life.

PART 3

The First Day of the Rest of Your Life: Bringing It All Together

CHAPTER 7

Getting Flexible: Finding Opportunities for Valued Living in Everyday Life

Now is the part where we consider how all the things you've practiced fit with each other, into the larger goal of psychological flexibility and the larger purpose of valued living. We start by pausing and checking out where we are and how we've found our way here.

WHERE WE'VE BEEN, WHAT WE'VE BROUGHT WITH US

Over the past four chapters, we've discussed different opportunities for psychological flexibility that can help make possible our commitments to valued living. And if you've stuck with the agenda, it's not been all talk (or all read, as the case may be). More important than the words you've read have been the changes you've made. At this point, you've practiced a whole host of new skills. To summarize, you've worked on:

- *Being present*, or noticing your ongoing experiences as they occur in and around you

- *Noticing self-as-context*, or contacting the "you" that is more than the things you know *about* you

- *Defusion,* or noticing your thoughts without letting certain thoughts dominate your experience

- *Accepting experience,* or being open to those thoughts and the feelings that come with them

And all of this you've done in service of your *commitment to valued living.* Whew.

If you're like us, then this has been hard work, the kind of work you've wanted to set down at times (maybe *most* times) and forget about. We'd like to take a moment and acknowledge that before moving on. Take a slow, deep breath and notice some of what has changed since you opened this book up the first time. See the things you've done differently out in the world in the moments when you've let go and stepped out of that stuck place. Notice where you've been since you read that first sentence. And breathe. See the things you've seen out in the world in the moments when you've slowed down enough to notice them. Notice the change you've brought with you. See the ways you're relating differently to your experiences. And breathe.

Before you go any further, we'd like to thank you for your work on this journey so far. That might seem like a funny thing to do since, as we said up front, we don't really know you. The part we do know, however, is the struggle we all share. Regardless of what it is we're fighting and what shape it takes in our lives, the struggle itself is something we know well. Who knows? The work you are doing here could be about more than the extraordinary changes you make in *your* life. It could be that opening yourself up to your experiences makes it easier for others to do so. It could be that moving about your world in a more purposeful way makes more room for others to find their way. Part of why we do this work is that we believe this to be true. Part of why we do this work is that we feel hopeful about what people could accomplish if they only let themselves. You have our gratitude and our deepest respect. Thank you.

And now... back to the job.

Four Opportunities, One Valued Practice

One thing you may be noticing as you get further into this work is that the opportunities for psychological flexibility don't feel all that different from the inside out. The definitions might sound pretty different, and the practices have different instructions. But part of what you may have noticed about this work is that the practices sort of seeped together. You probably found yourself carrying things you learned in chapter 3 into your later practices. In fact, if you think back, it may be hard to remember which exercises focused on what.

Turns out that that's not much of a problem. Being present, noticing self-as-context, defusion, and acceptance feel like they tap into the same process because they do. Remember, the deal with these different skills is that they are all facets of the same thing—psychological flexibility. And not only that, these are all opportunities *for* the same thing—valued living.

Maybe you just can't practice one aspect of psychological flexibility without practicing the others. For example, it's hard to be accepting of something that you aren't present to experience. Acceptance always requires at least a little bit of being present. It's hard to contact yourself as a context for feelings if you aren't willing to feel. Self-as-context is easiest with a little bit of acceptance. And none of these mean much of anything outside of how they help you toward valued living.

One in the Context of Many

The practices we described targeted different experiences, but you could easily build on any of these to address each of the opportunities for psychological flexibility. For example, you could start with any being-present exercise and gently move into noticing fused thoughts, then defusing, then saying yes to even those thoughts, then noticing the self as the part of you that held all of those experiences. In some ways, these are not different practices, but one practice, with different opportunities within that practice.

We encourage you to take some time and thumb through some of the earlier chapters. Redo a couple of the exercises in different chapters, noticing how they feel different now. Practicing being present may go differently now that you've learned to recognize your perspective, or to defuse, or to accept your experience. The same is true of any of the opportunities we've discussed. And another thing—when you notice yourself rushing past some of the practices, relieved to turn the page on them, it may be worth it to pause and settle into those very ones. Remember the backward compass. Often the directions from which we want to turn are the very ones in which something precious might lie.

So, pick a few practices to redo. Choose the ones that were the most meaningful or the most difficult, or the ones that affected you most. Record your experiences below.

Name of Practice	Comments (for example, what did you notice? What, if anything, was different this time?)

What did you notice? Are you surprised by what has changed?

The Job

If the opportunities you spent all that time practicing are really all pieces of the same thing, it might be hard to see why we even bother to describe them as separate. We've made a point to explain the different opportunities for valued living because this allows us to target specific struggles. The idea is that everyone is psychologically inflexible. And this inflexibility interferes with everyone's lives in some way. We look to specific opportunities for valued living to find out *how* we are inflexible. I might find that my trouble with valued living is related to how hard it is for me to be present. You might see how it's always avoidance when you turn away. Once we know this, we can create a context for the practice of psychological flexibility. Once we know this, we can create a context for a valued life to be built.

And here's our big secret (you might not like it...): the job isn't done. No matter how much you've practiced, your opportunities for valued living don't stop growing. No matter how hard you worked, you could still take one more step toward the life you want. What you're carrying with you now are not highly specialized skills that will allow you to remain always present, always in touch with self, always defused, and always accepting. And we wouldn't want that for you anyway. What you're carrying with you is a new perspective through which you might see opportunities where there formerly were none.

We've given you opportunities to practice these skills not because we think you can now pocket them for perfect use when you need them. We hope, instead, that you can see your struggle more clearly both now and in the moment that you find yourself. We hope that you can notice how you participate in that struggle and see opportunities for change. We hope that you can approach yourself gently and with the support you need to stretch and grow in new directions.

In other words, it's less like we've given you a wrench and taught you to tighten gadget bolts that come loose, and more like we've given you a lesson on how the gadget works. Our idea is that if you know how all this works, not only can you fix it when things go haywire, but you can adjust it to whatever it is you're trying to do.

THE LIFE YOU'RE BUILDING

And what *are* you trying to do? Not just today. Not just right now. On a large scale. What is the life that you're trying to build? It's a big question. A hard question. One you might not feel quite ready to answer. A question whose answer will certainly change over time. A question whose answer can't be judged as to accuracy, only as to choice. Your "wrong" life is the one you didn't and aren't choosing—the one you barely notice you are building as the walls come up closer and closer around you.

You know, you already started to answer this question when you filled out the Valued Living Questionnaire in chapter 2 and chose something for this work to be about. When you chose valued practices, chapter after chapter. And now. Slowly, brick by brick, you began building the life you choose. And it hasn't gotten any easier.

Valuing may be a little different now that you've spent some time practicing being present, self-as-context, defusion, and acceptance. You may notice things you missed along the way. You may see values you wrote down because they felt like the next line in your story. You may notice moments when your thoughts became more important than what you were trying to accomplish. You may recognize the ways you held back or played it safe to keep from getting hurt or being disappointed.

And as we've said over and over throughout this book, commitment to valued living is not about never missing things, or never turning away, or never holding back. Commitment is about noticing when you've moved away from values, then coming back to the table. So take a moment now and look over the valued practices you've committed to throughout the course of this book. Read each one to yourself slowly. Notice the thoughts and feelings that come up as you consider the commitments you've made. Notice the thoughts and feelings that come up as you consider the commitments you turned away from. And breathe.

What shape might your valued living take after your journey with us is over? How might committed valued living look over the course of the next week? The next month? How might your values play out over the next year? The next ten years? Twenty? Notice your mind wanting to figure this out, to get some good answers to these questions. Notice this and see if you can't simply linger in the questions, without rushing into any answers.

VALUED PRACTICE
(GUIDED MEDITATION)

Values are not the kinds of things that we eventually accomplish, wiping our hands off with a smirk while admirers say, "Good show!" They are the kinds of things we struggle with most times for just those few moments of sweetness. It is useful, from time to time, to pause and carefully consider different aspects of our lives.

We invite you now to bring the open, defused, and accepting perspectives you've been practicing to bear on your life as a whole. We'll ask you to consider different domains of your life, noticing the sad and the sweet, the struggle and the stillness. This will be, by far, the longest practice we've done so far. We encourage you to set aside at least thirty minutes of uninterrupted time. It may not take the whole time to complete, but having that protected time will ensure that you get the most out of it. Note: this practice is available as a download but is not on the CD.

- First, let your eyes close and see if you can just breathe in the experience of being here in this room right now. Sit up straight in your chair with your head balanced at the top of your spine, allowing your shoulders to drop and the muscles in your face to relax.

- Take a moment and just let your attention come to rest right now on the gentle inflow and outflow of breath.

- And if you find yourself thinking forward to what we are doing, gently let go of that and notice again that in the midst of all that mental activity, your breath continues. No matter how busy you get, it is there, flowing like a river. It requires nothing of you.

- Just let yourself linger for a moment inside that steady stream of inflow and outflow of breath. Each time you find yourself drifting away in thought, into the future or past, just let that steady inflow and outflow draw your attention gently back. Allow yourself to just notice all of the tiny sensations: in your lips, in your mouth, the gentle rise and fall of your own breath. Returning each time you drift gently back to your own breath.

- And if you find yourself irritated, wanting to move along, just notice that—that push—and imagine that you just gently release that and come back to this very next breath…and this breath.

- Now you will ask yourself a series of questions about areas of life that some people value. Some of these areas may be very important to you. Others may not. It is not necessary that you value all areas. Just read or listen to the questions, repeat them to yourself, and allow yourself to sit for a moment with each question. Even if the area is not one that is important to you, just let yourself be curious about the question.

- As you move through the questions, notice any thoughts, feelings, sensations, or memories that come up for you. Take a moment to breathe them in and out, then gently release them. These are important areas of living and we don't always pause and give ourselves time to appreciate them.

- It's not important right now to answer these questions. Just imagine that asking yourself these questions was like dipping into a pool of water. Just let the questions soak in. And breathe.

- If you find yourself drawing any conclusions, just gently let go of those conclusions and return your attention to the question.

- As you notice your reactions, let go of the urge to understand them, judge them, grip onto them, or push them away. When you notice your reactions, just breathe that experience in, and on the next exhale, slowly set it aside and see what shows up next.

FAMILY

Let's start with the area of family generally—outside of marriage and parenting.

- Read the following words slowly and let yourself settle into each of them, noticing whatever shows up:

    brother

    sister

    grandmother

    grandfather

granddaughter

grandson

cousin

aunt

uncle

niece

nephew

family

- Take a slow, deep breath and ask yourself, *If something were to happen in my life in the area of family, what would that mean to me? Are there people I would choose to reach out to? Is there a person in my family with whom I'd try to interact differently? What does it mean for me to be a son/daughter, a brother/sister? If I could be any kind of family member, what would I choose to be? What does family mean to me?*

- Linger inside of these questions, noticing any urges to rush through to the next section or to set this piece of the work down. And breathe.

- And, gently, breathe…just settle and allow your attention to come gently to rest on your own breath before shifting to another part of your life.

INTIMATE RELATIONS/COUPLES/MARRIAGE

- Read the following words slowly and let yourself settle into each of them, noticing whatever shows up:

partner

lover

couple

boyfriend

girlfriend

husband

wife

intimate

close

marriage

- Take a slow, deep breath and ask yourself, *If something were to happen in my life in the area of intimacy, what would that mean to me? Would I want to be with my partner in a new way? What does it mean for me to be a lover, a partner, a husband/wife? If I could choose any kind of partner to be, what would I choose?*

■ Linger inside of these questions, noticing any urges to rush through to the next section or to set this piece of the work down. And breathe.

■ And, gently, breathe…just settle and allow your attention to come gently to rest on your own breath before shifting to another part of your life.

PARENTING/SUPPORTING CHILDREN

■ Read the following words slowly and let yourself settle into each of them, noticing whatever shows up:

child

father

mother

mentor

leader

son

daughter

student

■ Take a slow, deep breath and ask yourself, *If something were to happen in my life in the area of support-ing children or parenting, what would that mean to me? Would I give more time and attention to a child whose life I'm in? Would I change the way I am with that child? Would I stand by a parent who could use some support? What does it mean to me to be in a child's life? If I could choose to be or help to support any kind of parent or mentor, what would I choose?*

■ Linger inside of these questions, noticing any urges to rush through to the next section or to set this piece of the work down. And breathe.

■ And, gently, breathe…just settle and allow your attention to come gently to rest on your own breath before shifting to another part of your life.

FRIENDSHIP/SOCIAL RELATIONS

■ Read the following words slowly and let yourself settle into each of them, noticing whatever shows up:

friend

buddy

companion

ally

supporter

helper

pal

- Take a slow, deep breath and ask yourself, *If something were to happen in my life in the area of friendship, what would that mean to me? What does it mean for me to be a friend? To have friends? If my friendships grew and changed, what shape might they take? Would old friendships be renewed; would new friendships grow? If I could be any kind of friend, what would I choose?*

- Linger inside of these questions, noticing any urges to rush through to the next section or to set this piece of the work down. And breathe.

- And, gently, breathe...just settle and allow your attention to come gently to rest on your own breath before shifting to another part of your life.

WORK/VOCATION

- Read the following words slowly and let yourself settle into each of them, noticing whatever shows up:

work

job

occupation

trade

career

vocation

profession

employee

worker

employer

boss

- Take a slow, deep breath and ask yourself, *If something were to happen in my life in the area of work, what would that mean to me? Would I find new life in the work I do? Would I stretch out into the work that I've wanted but kept myself from moving toward? If I could be any kind of worker, what kind would I be?*

- Linger inside of these questions, noticing any urges to rush through to the next section or to set this piece of the work down. And breathe.

- And, gently, breathe...just settle and allow your attention to come gently to rest on your own breath before shifting to another part of your life.

EDUCATION/TRAINING

■ Read the following words slowly and let yourself settle into each of them, noticing whatever shows up:

student

learning

school

class

teacher

growth

■ Take a slow, deep breath and ask yourself, *If something were to happen in my life in the area of educa-tion, of learning something new or learning more in some area that I care about, what would that mean to me? Would I find meaning and new life in learning? Would I stretch out into the education or training that I've wanted but kept myself from moving toward? If I could be any kind of student, what kind would I be?*

■ Linger inside of these questions, noticing any urges to rush through to the next section or to set this piece of the work down. And breathe.

■ And, gently, breathe…just settle and allow your attention to come gently to rest on your own breath before shifting to another part of your life.

RECREATION

■ Read the following words slowly and let yourself settle into each of them, noticing whatever shows up:

fun

relaxation

recreation

leisure

enjoyment

hobby

rest

sport

vacation

peace

■ Take a slow, deep breath and ask yourself, *If something were to happen in my life in the area of recreation, of giving myself relaxation or peace, what would that mean to me? Would I find new life in a hobby or sport?*

Would I return to an activity I've let go of that used to be meaningful to me? Would I stretch out into an activity that I've wanted to do by kept myself from doing?

- Linger inside of these questions, noticing any urges to rush through to the next section or to set this piece of the work down. And breathe.

- And, gently, breathe…just settle and allow your attention to come gently to rest on your own breath before shifting to another part of your life.

SPIRITUALITY

- Read the following words slowly and let yourself settle into each of them, noticing whatever shows up:

  spirituality

  sacred

  religion

  faith

  holy

  reverence

  ritual

- Take a slow, deep breath and ask yourself, *If something were to happen in my life in the area of spirituality, of building something sacred into my world, what would that mean to me? Would I return to a faith I've let go of that used to be meaningful to me? Would I reach out for the spiritual practice that I've wanted but kept myself from moving toward? If I could be any kind of spiritual person, what kind of person would I choose to be?*

- Linger inside of these questions, noticing any urges to rush through to the next section or to set this piece of the work down. And breathe.

- And, gently, breathe…just settle and allow your attention to come gently to rest on your own breath before shifting to another part of your life.

COMMUNITY LIFE

- Read the following words slowly and let yourself settle into each of them, noticing whatever shows up:

  community

  group

  club

  member

citizen

neighbor

helper

volunteer

representative

resident

■ Take a slow, deep breath and ask yourself, *If something were to happen in my life in the area of my community, what would that mean to me? Would I find a new group of people that represent the things I do or believe? Would I turn back to a group I was active with in the past? If I could choose to be any kind of community member, what kind would I be?*

■ Linger inside of these questions, noticing any urges to rush through to the next section or to set this piece of the work down. And breathe.

■ And, gently, breathe...just settle and allow your attention to come gently to rest on your own breath before shifting to another part of your life.

HEALTH AND SELF-CARE

■ Read the following words slowly and let yourself settle into each of them, noticing whatever shows up:

healthy

fit

strong

well

alive

energetic

vigorous

■ Take a slow, deep breath and ask yourself, *If something were to happen in my life in the area of my health and self-care, what would that mean to me? Would I take care of myself in a way I never have before? Would I set down something I do that hurts me? If I could choose to be a caretaker of my body, what kind would I be?*

■ Linger inside of these questions, noticing any urges to rush through to the next section or to set this piece of the work down. And breathe.

■ And, gently, breathe...just settle and allow your attention to come gently to rest on your own breath before shifting to another part of your life.

THE ENVIRONMENT

▨ Read the following words slowly and let yourself settle into each of them, noticing whatever shows up:

nature

Earth

the environment

ecosystems

life

▨ Take a slow, deep breath and ask yourself, *If something were to happen in my life in the area of my relationship with the environment, what would that mean to me? Would I care for the Earth in a way I never have before? Would I let go of things that I do that damage the environment? If I could choose to be a caretaker of the world around me, what kind would I choose to be?*

▨ Linger inside of these questions, noticing any urges to rush through to the next section or to set this piece of the work down. And breathe.

▨ And, gently, breathe…just settle and allow your attention to come gently to rest on your own breath before shifting to another part of your life.

BEAUTY/THE ARTS

▨ Read the following words slowly and let yourself settle into each of them, noticing whatever shows up:

beauty

art

theatre

music

literature

creativity

appreciation

expression

▨ Take a slow, deep breath and ask yourself, *If something were to happen in my life in the area of my relationship with beauty and the arts, what would that mean to me? Would I look at the world a little differently than I have been? Would I take more time for creative expression? If I could choose to see, appreciate, and express the beauty of the world around me, how would I choose to do that?*

- Linger inside of these questions, noticing any urges to rush through to the next section or to set this piece of the work down. And breathe.

- And, gently, breathe…just settle and allow your attention to come gently to rest on your own breath.

CONCLUSION

- Let your awareness touch once more on each of these areas: intimate relations, parenting, family, friendship, work, education, recreation, spirituality, community, self-care, the environment, and the arts.

- Notice any urges to skip certain areas of life or to rush through the end of this practice. See if you can't breathe that urge in and out.

- Without opening your eyes, call your attention gently back to your own body here in this room right now.

- We invite you to open your eyes in just a moment and take just a few minutes to write about what shows up for you as the most important thing or things in your life, and why this is important and meaningful to you. Write your deepest thoughts and feelings about this area of living. What you write does not have to be grammatically correct. Don't worry about spelling or even necessarily writing in complete sentences.

- Open your eyes and set your timer for ten minutes. Please write for the entire ten minutes. If you cannot think of what else you might say, just rewrite the last thing you wrote over and over until something new comes up. If you run out of room in this book, continue on a separate sheet of paper.

_____

_____

_____

_____

_____

_____

_____

_____

_____

_____

_____

_____

_____

_____

_____

_____

_____

_____

_____

_____

_____

_____

_____

_____

_____

_____

And now, without taking a break, we invite you to take a few moments and complete another Valued Living Questionnaire, without letting go of the practice you just completed as you rate these areas of your life according to possibility, importance, action, satisfaction, and concern.

VALUED LIVING QUESTIONNAIRE

Below are areas of life that are valued by some people. We are concerned with your quality of life in each of these areas. You'll rate several aspects in regard to each area. Ask yourself the following questions when you make ratings in each area. Not everyone will value all of these areas or value all areas the same. Rate each area according to your own personal view.

Possibility: How possible is it that something very meaningful could happen in this area of your life? Rate how possible you think it is on a scale of 1 to 10. 1 means that it isn't at all possible and 10 means that it is very possible.

Current importance: How important is this area at this time in your life? Rate the importance on a scale of 1 to 10. 1 means the area isn't at all important and 10 means the area is very important.

Overall importance: How important is this area in your life as a whole? Rate the importance on a scale of 1 to 10. 1 means that the area isn't at all important and 10 means that the area is very important.

Action: How much have you acted in the service of this area during the past week? Rate your level of action on a scale of 1 to 10. 1 means you haven't been active at all with this value and 10 means you've been very active with this value.

Satisfied with level of action: How satisfied are you with your level of action in this area during the past week? Rate your satisfaction with your level of action on a scale of 1 to 10. 1 means you aren't at all satisfied and 10 means you're completely satisfied with your level of action in this area.

Concern: How concerned are you that this area won't progress as you want? Rate your level of concern on a scale of 1 to 10. 1 means that you aren't at all concerned and 10 means that you're very concerned.

	Possibility	Current Impor- tance	Overall Impor- tance	Action	Satisfied with Action	Concern
1. Family (other than marriage or parenting)						
2. Marriage, Couples, or Intimate relations						
3. Parenting						
4. Friends and Social Life						
5. Work						
6. Education and Training						
7. Recreation and Fun						
8. Spirituality						
9. Community Life						

10. Physical Self-Care (diet, exercise, and sleep)						
11. The Environment (caring for the planet)						
12. Aesthetics (art, literature, music, beauty)						

And now, give yourself a break. Seriously. Put this book down for a while before moving on to our final chapter. Wait, wait, wait… Hold on! You're not totally off the hook. During your break, we encourage you to keep one hand on the experiences you've had here in this last practice. Notice opportunities in your everyday life for committed action across the areas of life you considered here. Even in areas of your life that aren't particularly important to you, it may be beneficial to notice that if they were important, you could serve that value by taking (or letting go of) a particular action. Let yourself wonder about taking this action or that. What would it be like? Pay special attention to the moments when you notice yourself turning away from valued living. Ask yourself, "What would turning back look like in this moment?" And note—we're not asking you to do anything in particular except notice places where you could take one more step on your valued path, where you could lay one more brick toward building your valued life. And finally, notice which of those opportunities you take, which you don't, and the effect of those choices.

CHAPTER 8

One Step at a Time: Choosing Committed Action

Well? Did you take your break? And on your break did you "notice places where you could take one more step on your valued path"? Did you "notice which of those opportunities you take, which you don't, and the effect of those choices"? (Didn't think we'd ask about it, did you?)

If you're like most people, the answer ranges from "not really" to "sort of." Some moments you did. You settled into what was going on around you and noticed all of the possibilities for valued action. And some moments you didn't. You were busy or distracted or upset or overwhelmed, and you didn't do the job. Until you did again. Depending on how long of a break you took, you may have gone back and forth between noticing and not noticing a number of times before picking this book up again. But if you're reading this, one thing is certain—you came back to the work.

Most things that matter to us are like this. We spend some time on the job, and some time off the job. Sometimes we can tell how much things matter to us by how much time and energy we spend on them. We see somebody starting to slack off at something and it seems obvious that they don't care about it. Sometimes, however, it's exactly the opposite. Sometimes we care about something so much that we can hardly bear the thought of it not working out like we want it to. And a day comes eventually when we get lost, or we screw up, or the job in front of us just seems too hard, and we turn away. And turning back to a thing that matters to us as much as anything is that much harder because now we have to face more than just the risk that we might lose it. We have to face the fact that we turned away and everything that that seems to mean. So we avoid a little longer. And the longer we stay turned away, the harder it is to turn back.

THE GENTLE TURN BACK

From an ACT perspective, this is precisely where commitment comes in. Not beforehand, as you look out at that valued path, hold your breath, cross your fingers, and take that first step, but when you find yourself having gone astray. In that moment when you suddenly realize how nothing in front of you looks like the life you wanted, the thing to do is pause, look around, and gently turn back.

We've asked you to make commitments in every chapter of this book—to think of and commit to ways to apply this flexibility stuff in your life. And again, what made them commitments was not how you said you were going to do something, how you thought it over and wrote it down in the blank. It was when you realized you were zoning out at your grandmother's birthday party, so you paused, took a deep breath, and noticed the sun in her hair or the shame in your heart. That's turning back. That's commitment.

Now we'll ask you to make a few more commitments. These commitments are part of what you'll carry with you when you read the last word on the last page of this book, close the book, and set it down. These are commitments about the ways that you will continue to bring psychological flexibility to bear in your life. These are commitments about what you'll turn back to in the moments you find yourself lost.

PRACTICE: BABY STEPS, GIANT LEAPS (GUIDED PRACTICE)

- Take three slow, deep breaths, letting yourself notice what it feels like to breathe. Notice the sensations that come with breathing. Notice the air rushing by your nose and lips, the muscles in your chest and abdomen pumping air in and out, the heaviness that grows in your arms and legs. And breathe.

- When you feel yourself sort of settled in, turn back to the Valued Living Questionnaire that you completed at the end of the last chapter. Take a moment to read over the questionnaire, reminding yourself of the areas of life it asks about and of what the different rating scales mean. And breathe.

- Let your attention come to rest on the column marked "Current Importance." Scan the ratings you marked there. Find the area of life you marked with the lowest rating, then the one you marked with the next lowest rating, and so on. Settle your attention upon the areas of life you rated the highest. And breathe.

- Name these areas of life that are most important to you one at a time. Name them quietly, but out loud. As you name each area of life, call to mind what it means to you. If you notice that some are harder to take time with than others, just notice that, and turn gently back to that one more time before moving on. And breathe.

■ Now shift your attention gently to the columns marked "Action" and "Satisfaction with Action." Notice the level of action you indicated and how satisfied you said you were with that. Pay special attention to the areas you said were most important to you. And breathe.

■ Let your attention settle on three areas that you value but in which you have not been satisfied with the actions you've been taking. If there's another area of life for which this fits, but it's not listed on the VLQ-II, let that be one of your three. And breathe.

■ Record those three values below:

I value _____.

I value _____.

I value _____.

■ Now call to mind these values one at a time. See yourself in moments in which you turned away from these values. Notice any urges to rush through this part or to skip it. Take a slow, deep breath, and return your attention to examples of what turning away looks like for you. And breathe.

■ Settle upon one example of how you've turned away for each of them. Record those below:

I've turned away from my value of _____ by

_____.

I've turned away from my value of _____ by

_____.

I've turned away from my value of _____ by

_____.

■ Now, imagine that you could take three small actions today or tomorrow that would shift you gently back toward these things you really care about. These can be any actions that you think fit with your value as you see it. Keep it small, though. Take the first things that come to you and push to think of some actions even smaller than that. And breathe.

■ Jot down what those commitments to perform three tiny valued actions might look like:

I could commit to serving my value of _____ by

_____.

I could commit to serving my value of _____ by

_____ .

I could commit to serving my value of _____ by

_____ .

- Slowly read over the possible commitments you wrote. Imagine yourself carrying out these actions. Make up as many details as you can and watch yourself doing these things from start to finish.

- Notice what comes up for you. Notice any judgment or guilt or disappointment or sadness that shows up. And if you find yourself turning away from these, see if you can't turn gently back. Breathe the judgment or guilt or disappointment or sadness in and out slowly. Notice if this feels familiar. Notice if these are part of what you've turned away from before. And breathe.

- Now imagine that you could take giant leaps in each of these three areas. Maybe not right now, maybe not next week, but at some point you could take a deep breath and make a bold move that would put you somewhere that you feel is way out of reach right now.

- Jot down what those commitments to perform three tiny valued actions might look like:

I could commit to serving my value of _____ by

_____ .

I could commit to serving my value of _____ by

_____ .

I could commit to serving my value of _____ by

_____ .

- Slowly read over the possible commitments you wrote. Imagine yourself carrying out these actions. Make up as many details as you can, and watch yourself doing these things from start to finish.

- Notice what comes up for you. Notice any judgment or doubt or regret or fear that shows up. And if you find yourself turning away from these, see if you can't turn gently back. Breathe the judgment or doubt or regret or fear in and out slowly. Notice if this feels familiar. Notice if these are part of what you've turned away from before. And breathe.

- Finally, take three slow, deep breaths, noticing once more that now-familiar sensation of breathing.

You may have noticed that you didn't seem to actually make any commitments. You didn't promise to do this or that. You just sort of considered them, imagined yourself carrying them out, and noticed what might be holding you back. Now, we didn't have you do this because we think that visualization exerts any kind of power over the universe to make these things occur. We do think, however, that this is practicing something different from what has been happening in your life. You might hear of an opportunity, start to feel hopeful for a minute, and then, close behind that hope, feel doubt or fear or regret. And often, in that moment, you turn away. In other words, commitment, as a practice, might start with the gentle turns back that others might not even be able to see. What if commitment begins with the moments in which we dare to wonder, or dream, or hope, even in the face of doubt and fear and regret?

PRACTICE: WONDERING, HOPING, AND DREAMING

Call to mind a specific valued area of your life in which you've avoided wondering, hoping, and dreaming about what might be possible. We invite you to make a specific commitment to wonder, hope, and dream about the things that matter to you. For example, you might commit to wondering about what continuing your education might be like. You might commit to hoping for more from your friendships. You might commit to dreaming about physical achievements, like running a marathon. List as many possibilities for wondering, hoping, and dreaming as you can think of, using another page if necessary.

I commit to wondering, hoping, and dreaming about:

1. _____

2. _____

3. _____

4. _____

5. _____

6. _____

7. _____

8. _____

9. _____

10. _____

11. _____

12. _____

13. _____

14. _____

15. _____

16. _____

17. _____

18. _____

19. _____

20. _____

21. _____

22. _____

23. _____

24. _____

25. _____

26. _____

27. _____

28. _____

29. _____

30. _____

Don't forget about this list. Come back to it every now and then. Put it on the refrigerator. Copy it ten times and hide it around the house. Most importantly, add to it. You'll never choose to make changes that you won't even let yourself wonder about first.

SEEKING SUPPORTIVE RESOURCES: BUILDING THE CONTEXT FOR CHANGE

As you've started to make changes in your life with this piece of work, you've undoubtedly noticed that change is just not easy. We humans don't really tend to let go of things we learn once we learn them. Think about those things you do that you hate. At the worst times, you watch yourself doing *that thing you do* like a car accident, dimly aware of how badly this is certain to turn out. Even things we do that we would just as soon forget about tend to hang on, undetected, until the moment when we're taking a beating. Suddenly there we are, hurting ourselves or someone we care about, and not seeing any other way out.

Why is change so hard? We discussed way back in chapter 2 how we understand behavior as being learned in and maintained by the context. Part of what makes change so hard is that it requires that either the context change or the relationship between the behavior and the context change. In ACT, we focus mostly on changing the relationship. We can't make the contexts you carry with you go away for good, and we don't want you squeezing down your life to avoid hard situations. So we focus on the relationship by calling up the context (for example, painful thoughts and feelings) and practicing new behavior in its presence.

For example, if you want to stop binge eating and you binge eat whenever you experience stress, removing stress would be one way to stop binge eating—except that efforts to make stress go away often end up resulting in more stress. Another way to change binge eating would be to practice doing other things when stress is present. In ACT, this involves practicing being present, noticing self-as-context, defusing, and accepting when stress is present in order to make binge eating less likely.

You can, however, adjust some of your external context to support the changes you've made in this piece of work. In other words, the next step for you might be building some context for valued living to continue. This might include talking to family and friends about what you're trying to do, working with a therapist or counselor, seeking other resources for additional support, and continuing to use this book.

Talking to Family and Friends

We started every chapter in this book by describing how things that we all do (such as avoid hurt) can cause problems in our lives. Presumably your friends and family struggle like everyone else. And they probably haven't thought much about an alternative.

This can make it tough not to fall back into the way things have always been. Let's face it: if your social context supported being present, noticing self-as-context, defusing, and accepting, you probably wouldn't have needed this book in the first place. With this in mind, some people choose to talk to their friends and family about their attempt to let go of this struggle with eating and body image. So how do you talk to the people in your life about changes you're making? How do you help them to understand an approach that you're just beginning to understand yourself? This is rarely an easy conversation. We do, however, have a couple of tips.

First, we encourage you to decide before a conversation like this what you are hoping to get out of it. Watch out for the conversations that feel worth it only if you get a particular response. In these cases, it might be best to hold off. You can't always count on others, no matter how much they love you or want to help, to know (and be willing to provide) what you are looking for. Pay special attention to the things that you'd value saying to the person, regardless of their response. These will make up your purpose for the conversation and will keep you on track when hard things start to show up.

Second, be ready to share specific ideas of how the person you're talking to could support you. What most of us know how to do when someone is hurting is help them avoid. We soothe, we try to show them the bright side, we give them things to do to try to feel better. Sharing your struggle with your loved ones is bound to result in some of this. When there are eating or body image struggles, it often involves people telling you "how beautiful you are" and how "you don't need to lose any weight!" If you're looking for support in building psychological flexibility, this kind of reaction is not going to be very helpful. But most people don't know what else to do to be supportive. So tell them. If there are specific things they can do, ask for those. For example, you might say something like, "Would you come with me to Pete's on Fridays to get a sandwich? It's good for me to practice just being there without fighting with myself the whole time."

Lastly, remember that the person doesn't have to get the whole idea in order to be helpful to you. It's hard sometimes not to want the people around us to know what we know and understand why we do what we do. But don't forget that they have their own struggles and their own ways of dealing with it. It can be overwhelming to try to learn about a completely new way to be. You remember! It would be easy for someone to feel like you were saying they had to agree with your ideas (or maybe even change themselves) in order to be supportive to you. You can make this less likely by describing these changes as something you are choosing (as opposed to "the right thing," or what people "should do"). For example, you might have a friend suggest that if you just think positively you'll feel better. It might be useful to reply, "You know, at this point, I'm not even fighting the thoughts... I'm just focusing on the things that matter more to me than that." In this way, your loved one doesn't have to be wrong to be helpful.

Now, all that being said, there might not be anyone in your life with whom you value sharing this work. And that may change. Or it may not. The thing to do is allow yourself to notice if this is something that would serve your values. Even if you are thinking, "No way could anyone in my life handle this kind of conversation," take a moment here and now to entertain the possibility.

Other ACT Resources

If you've taken to the ACT approach and feel you've benefited from the structure of the practices we offered in this book, you might want to pick up another ACT workbook. Every book describes the ACT perspective a little differently and includes different ways of practicing psychological flexibility. It may be that things you are still a bit fuzzy on would clear up completely with a different example, metaphor, or exercise.

Steven C. Hayes's workbook with Spencer Smith, *Get Out of Your Mind and Into Your Life: The New Acceptance and Commitment Therapy* (New Harbinger 2005), offers an introduction to ACT that doesn't focus on any one kind of diagnosis or problem. If you want something specific to eating problems, Michelle Heffner and Georg H. Eifert wrote *The Anorexia Workbook: How to Accept Yourself,*

Heal Your Suffering, and Reclaim Your Life (New Harbinger 2004), which focuses more on the kinds of problems that come with self-starvation and being underweight. Finally, if you want to read more about what *we* have to say on this topic, the three of us have just begun another workbook that focuses on body image problems that should be released in 2012.

If your interest in ACT moves from practical to intellectual, there are also books on these same topics available for professionals. As we write this, our professionally focused book, *Acceptance and Commitment Therapy for Eating Disorders* (New Harbinger 2011), is progressing through its final edit. It's quite a bit more technical than this one, digging deeply into the theory and basic behavioral science that underlies this work. If you find yourself intrigued by the ACT perspective, however, it may be worth taking a look.

Finally, you may pay a visit to the website for the Association for Contextual Behavioral Science, or ACBS. Unlike most professional association websites, ACBS maintains all kinds of different resources for folks who aren't professionals. A good place to start is the "ACT for the Public" page at www.contextual psychology.org/act_for_the_public. This page offers links to more self-help resources, information about the theory and research behind ACT, ACT-relevant articles, videos, and interviews, as well as tips on how to find an ACT therapist and join the e-mail discussion list.

Continuing to Use This Book

Finally, even though you're reaching the end, there's no reason you can't continue to use this book and the accompanying audio tracks. As you may have noticed, no two meditations are ever the same. Even if you're using the same audio track, meditation is a new experience each time. As for the book, none of the paper-pencil practices are things you couldn't do on a notebook page, a sticky note, or a napkin. And even the same explanations and metaphors will speak to you differently on different days. For some of us, books are not the kinds of things you ever "finish." We'd be delighted if this book were to become a well-worn addition to your shelf.

YET ANOTHER INVITATION

At the beginning of this book we offered you an invitation to accompany us on a journey. We didn't tell you what to expect, but hopefully, you found something meaningful inside of it. Now we've come to the end of our time together. And so we offer one more invitation: we respectfully request your presence in the rest of your life. Go out and be. Slow down and notice. Welcome the hurt and the joy. Live your values. Commit to some stuff. We'll be here with our hopes for you, even in the moments you let go of your own.

References

Baumeister, R. F., J. D. Campbell, J. I. Krueger, and K. D. Vohs. 2003. Does high self-esteem cause better performance, interpersonal success, happiness, or healthier lifestyles? *Psychological Science in the Public Interest* 4:1–44.

Giambra, L. 2000. Daydreaming characteristics across the life-span: Age differences and seven to twenty year longitudinal changes. In *Individual Differences in Conscious Experience Ins.* Amsterdam: John Benjamins Publishing Company.

Hayes, S. C. 1984. Making sense of spirituality. *Behaviorism* 12:99–110.

Hayes, S. C., K. D. Strosahl, and K. G. Wilson. 1999. *Acceptance and Commitment Therapy: An Experiential Approach to Behavior Change.* New York: The Guilford Press.

Kane, M. J., L. H. Brown, J. C. McVay, P. J. Silvia, I. Myin-Germeys, and T. R. Kwapil. 2007. For whom the mind wanders, and when: An experience-sampling study of working memory and executive control in daily life. *Psychological Science* 18:614–621.

Melnyk, S. E., T. F. Cash, and L. H. Janda. 2004. Body image ups and downs: Prediction of intra-individual level and variability of women's daily body image experiences. *Body Image* 1:225–235.

Vilardaga, R. 2009. A relational frame theory account of empathy. *International Journal of Behavioral Consultation and Therapy* 5:178–184.

Emily K. Sandoz, PhD, is assistant professor of psychology at University of Louisiana at Lafayette and coauthor of *Acceptance and Commitment Therapy for Eating Disorders*. She is a clinical psychologist and behavior analyst who specializes in treating clients using acceptance and commitment therapy. She lives and works in Lafayette, LA.

Kelly G. Wilson, PhD, is associate professor of psychology at the University of Mississippi. He is coauthor of *Acceptance and Commitment Therapy, Mindfulness for Two, Things Might Go Terribly, Horribly Wrong,* and *Acceptance and Commitment Therapy for Eating Disorders*. He is a popular trainer and speaker in the areas of acceptance and commitment therapy and behavior analysis, with a busy schedule of national and international engagements. Wilson lives and works in Oxford, MS. www.onelifellc.com.

Troy DuFrene is a writer in the San Francisco Bay Area who specializes in psychology. He is coauthor of *Coping with OCD, Mindfulness for Two, Things Might Go Terribly, Horribly Wrong,* and *Acceptance and Commitment Therapy for Eating Disorders*. www.troydufrene.com

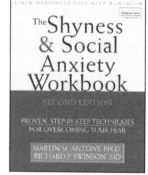